The AI Organization

Learn from Real Companies and Microsoft's Journey How to Redefine Your Organization with AI

David Carmona

Beijing · Boston · Farnham · Sebastopol · Tokyo

The AI Organization

by David Carmona

Copyright © 2020 David Carmona. All rights reserved.

Published by O'Reilly Media, Inc., 1005 Gravenstein Highway North, Sebastopol, CA 95472.

O'Reilly books may be purchased for educational, business, or sales promotional use. Online editions are also available for most titles (*http://oreilly.com*). For more information, contact our corporate/institutional sales department: 800-998-9938 or *corporate@oreilly.com*.

Acquisitions Editor: Melissa Duffield	**Indexer:** Ellen Troutman-Zaig
Developmental Editor: Alicia Young	**Interior Designer:** Monica Kamsvaag
Production Editor: Kristen Brown	**Cover Designer:** Randy Comer
Copyeditor: Rachel Head	**Illustrator:** Rebecca Demarest
Proofreader: Octal Publishing, LLC	

November 2019:   First Edition

Revision History for the First Edition

2019-11-12:   First Release

See *http://oreilly.com/catalog/errata.csp?isbn=9781492057376* for release details.

The O'Reilly logo is a registered trademark of O'Reilly Media, Inc. *The AI Organization*, the cover image, and related trade dress are trademarks of O'Reilly Media, Inc.

978-1-492-05737-6

[LSI]

To the family I was lucky to be born to in Cádiz,
the Microsoft family that adopted me in Redmond,
and the family I love with all my heart: Esther, Marcos, Guillermo, and Angela.

Contents

Preface

Have you ever been waiting for something to happen so impatiently that you counted down the days? I took that to the next level when I was eight. I still remember waiting for my first computer to arrive—a Commodore 64. Not only was I counting the days left, but I actually had dreams involving a time machine that I used for the sole purpose of fast-forwarding through those few days and making the wait shorter. I suppose that was my first exercise in overengineering.

My world expanded when the computer finally arrived. It wasn't like any toy I'd ever seen; you could actually provide the instructions to make it do whatever you wanted. As I learned BASIC, my universe kept expanding. I still remember my cousin showing me how to store text strings by adding a simple dollar sign to a variable. I didn't believe it—suddenly I could make the machine have a conversation with humans! After many if-then-elses, I called my father and excitedly told him to ask the machine a question. It didn't work, of course; he would have needed to say exactly one of the sentences I'd programmed in my code. Unfortunately, my cousin didn't know about things like machine learning, neural networks, or natural language processing. Almost nobody did at that time.

Fast-forward 15 years. Now in college, I had the opportunity to learn about all of these exciting concepts. I couldn't wait to put my newfound knowledge into practice—the idea of teaching a machine by examples instead of manually providing the instructions to perform an action was mind blowing. I decided to use machine learning techniques to complete an exam assignment involving a robotic arm equipped with a camera and a marker. The system should have been able to play tic-tac-toe with a human, identifying the board state on a piece of paper, working out the best next move, and physically drawing the move on the paper. It was a disaster.

Using techniques like neural networks for such a project at that time was just not practical: the functionality for accomplishing tasks like object detection to identify the board and the marks on it was not robust, and most computers available wouldn't have been powerful enough to run it anyway. I had to go back to if-then-elses to pass the exam and finish my college degree.

This mishap didn't affect my passion for computers, though. Well-written programs with thousands of if-then-elses and similar programming language constructs can still do amazing things. In my developer years after college I was able to create such diverse things as shareware applications, virtual reality 3D engines, software for tracking items in manufacturing production lines, and supervisory systems for power plants and airports, all of them requiring me to patiently add one instruction after the next.

During those times, I found a company whose products made my job easier. My connection with Microsoft was different than the connection many people had with it at that time, which was primarily focused on it operating systems. For me Microsoft was not the DOS or Windows company; it was the developer tools company. My beloved Commodore BASIC, which opened my world to computers, was actually based on Microsoft BASIC, the very first product of a tiny company at the time. As my career progressed, so did the tools I used. I discovered Microsoft Quick Basic, then the charming Visual Basic, which led to me embracing Visual Studio C++, and C# after that.

I was so in love with those products that helped developers create programs that I ended applying for a job at the company. I left my job creating applications to join Microsoft and help others creating those applications. That was 18 years ago. During that time I was fortunate enough to work in a group fully dedicated to helping developers and then to lead the business and marketing areas for my beloved Visual Studio, launching products such as Visual Studio Code, Visual Studio Online, and .NET Core. Never in my most amazing dreams would I have thought I would end up creating the kinds of tools that I had worshipped at the beginning of my career.

Then, a few years ago, something captured my attention. What had once seemed to be a dead end in software development was suddenly in the news again: advancements in neural networks from the research community and the vast compute power available in the cloud were providing amazing results. In 2015, a team at Microsoft Research developed a neural network so deep that it was able to identify images better than a human. And there was enough compute power available to run that neural network instantaneously. In a matter of months record-breaking results became common in the news: human parity was achieved on tasks like speech recognition, machine reading, and even translation.

All those achievements were made possible by the rebirth of artificial intelligence (AI).

As a developer, these achievements expanded my world once again. Just like the dollar sign my cousin had taught me all those years ago, AI techniques such as deep learning opened the door to entirely new scenarios. I didn't have to provide the instructions one by one; I could focus on designing an algorithm that could learn by itself. Applications that I had worked on before—like the chat program for my father or the tic-tac-toe robotic arm in college, or even the manufacturing monitoring or power plant software—could be redefined with these techniques and improved dramatically.

Career-wise, I made an important decision when this revolution started to happen. I left my beloved Developer Tools team and started to lead a newly created team at Microsoft for AI business and productization. Although my goal until then had been to help developers and organizations to program computers, my goal now is to help developers and organizations to *teach* computers. And at Microsoft, we are taking the same approach we took for programming: we are focusing on building the tools to make it easier for others to do this. Quoting my big boss, Satya Nadella, our work is to make others cool, not to be cool ourselves.

That approach has given me the opportunity to meet with hundreds of technical and business leaders from organizations around the globe that are in the process of embracing AI. From our perspective, we want to understand their needs so that we can provide the right solutions for them. But in practice, these are super-rich conversations in which we both share our learnings and the challenges we face.

I often get asked in these meetings about the difference between organizations that are embracing AI successfully and those that aren't. People are looking for the right organizational structure, the optimal use case, or the magic technology that can help them leverage the most important technological paradigm shift of this era.

I went through that mental process, too. I tried to get to the core of why some companies were more successful than others. And yes, I'll share those learnings in this book, including successful companies' organizational models, technologies, and use cases. You can use these learnings to shape your own strategy to embrace AI in your company. But beyond that, what I found behind these amazing companies was amazing people driven by a culture that empowered them. Just like the digital transformation that I was fortunate enough to experience through my customers, the AI transformation is driven by real people:

business leaders who have a vision; technical leaders who can translate it to technology; and developers, data scientists, and other employees who can make it a reality. And the connecting tissue across all of them is the culture ingrained in each of their organizations.

This book recounts my learnings from Microsoft's own transformation with AI, as well as from the companies I've worked with during my journey. You will also have the opportunity to go deeper into the technologies behind AI and even create your first applications yourself in the appendix of the book. But before that, you will learn about the strategies and culture of some of the successful companies I've encountered, as well as the heroes behind them. I was lucky enough to get to know some of these heroes and the personal stories that shaped them as leaders. You will find those stories intertwined with the chapters of this book, as introductions to the topics that follow—they're the cool ones, and I hope they will inspire you as they have me.

Conventions Used in This Book

The following typographical conventions are used in this book:

Italic

> Indicates new terms, URLs, email addresses, filenames, and file extensions.

`Constant width`

> Used for program listings, as well as within paragraphs to refer to program elements such as variable or function names, databases, data types, environment variables, statements, and keywords.

O'Reilly Online Learning

 For more than 40 years, *O'Reilly Media* has provided technology and business training, knowledge, and insight to help companies succeed.

Our unique network of experts and innovators share their knowledge and expertise through books, articles, conferences, and our online learning platform. O'Reilly's online learning platform gives you on-demand access to live training courses, in-depth learning paths, interactive coding environments, and a vast collection of text and video from O'Reilly and 200+ other publishers. For more information, please visit *http://oreilly.com*.

How to Contact Us

Please address comments and questions concerning this book to the publisher:

O'Reilly Media, Inc.
1005 Gravenstein Highway North
Sebastopol, CA 95472
800-998-9938 (in the United States or Canada)
707-829-0515 (international or local)
707-829-0104 (fax)

We have a web page for this book, where we list errata, examples, and any additional information. You can access this page at *https://oreil.ly/theAI-organization*.

Email *bookquestions@oreilly.com* to comment or ask technical questions about this book.

For more information about our books, courses, conferences, and news, see our website at *http://www.oreilly.com*.

Find us on Facebook: *http://facebook.com/oreilly*

Follow us on Twitter: *http://twitter.com/oreillymedia*

Watch us on YouTube: *http://www.youtube.com/oreillymedia*

AI Hero: Julián

When thinking about AI heroes, Julián (*https://oreil.ly/AIO_1a-1*) is the first person who comes to my mind. He doesn't have a PhD. He's not a regular speaker at AI research conferences. He hasn't published any papers or pioneered any core AI breakthroughs. Still, he represents the new wave of innovation that will truly transform the world we live in. The next big AI innovations will not only come from technology providers, but from industries like manufacturing, retail, banking, or—as in Julián's case—health care. These innovations will be driven by people who are connected to and knowledgeable about the problem domain, motivated to solve it, and empowered with democratized AI technologies.

Julián's motivation started in the middle of a Christmas holiday—the first one for his son Sergio, who was two months old at the time. When Julián heard his wife Lucía calling him to the bathroom he immediately knew something was wrong. That was the first time Sergio suffered a seizure episode, but unfortunately it wouldn't be the last.

Initially, Sergio had seizures once every two months, but soon they were happening up to eight times a day. Often, when Sergio had one of these episodes, his parents had to take him to the emergency room so that doctors could induce a coma to stop the seizing, while trying to prevent neurological damage.

We all have big expectations for modern medicine. In most cases, those expectations are well-founded—doctors are trained, based on hundreds of years of medical advancements, to diagnose diseases and treat them. That's the experience that most of us have with health care: we suffer a symptom, we go to the doctor, and we come back home with a diagnosis and a prescription to pick up at the pharmacy.

The experience for Sergio was far from that. Sergio suffered from a rare disease, and doctors were struggling to diagnose it. The first treatment, which would have worked for more common seizure cases, was actually making it worse, as they learned later. At one point he was suffering up to 20 seizures each day, an unbearable situation for him and his family.

Doctors are amazing professionals, but they have to rely on their training and experience to tackle the cases they encounter. That works great for the majority of diseases, but not for rare ones. Sergio saw multiple doctors over the course of eight months, and none of them were able to diagnose the condition he had—no medical professional can be an expert in every rare disease, and they simply could not find anyone who had knowledge of it.

Finally, Sergio was seen by a doctor who was able to identify his condition. He was diagnosed with Dravet syndrome, a rare and catastrophic form of epilepsy that begins in infancy and is associated with developmental and cognitive delays, movement and growth issues, and chronic infections, among other debilitating side effects.

Dravet syndrome is extremely rare, affecting just 1 in every 20,000 to 40,000 births. Most doctors will never have encountered it, and in most cases it takes years to diagnose. It is not curable, but seizures can be reduced with specific anticonvulsant medications, different than the ones Sergio was initially treated with. A specific diet, cognitive rehabilitation, and other treatments are also beneficial, and are all helping Sergio live a better life. Today, Sergio is 11 years old, and although he will be forever affected by his disease, the diagnosis helped his family to manage the symptoms and has improved his quality of life dramatically.

Julián's personal journey with relation to his son's condition was no different from any other parent's and is very well identified by psychology. Reality is different from movies, and when something like this happens the first reaction is not heroism and strength; it's desperation and paralysis, followed by adaptation.

But after those stages, we move into action. For Julián, that meant pivoting his life and having the determination to make a difference. Without any prior medical experience, Julián found himself learning more and more about his son's condition and the world of rare diseases, the complex human biology behind them, and the current approach of medicine to diagnosing them. With his technical background he saw a huge new world of possibilities—especially with the early buzz at that time surrounding the latest advances in AI.

Approximately 80% of rare diseases are genetic and caused by a mutation. Genetic mutations are the foundation of the evolution of species and the reason we have evolved into what we are now, but they are inherently random. I love Julián's explanation of the effects of these mutations: he compares them to typos in the source code of a program. Adding, removing, or changing a random letter in a program can lead to very different results. Most of the mutations happen in source code comments, which don't have any impact on the program itself. The equivalent in genetics is a mutation happening in the noncoding regions of our DNA, called introns. Another possibility is for the typo to change a line of code that causes the program to fail in the compilation stage. Those types of changes are unfortunately also common in humans and cause a natural abortion. But another set of changes are more subtle, like changing the value of a variable, and can be "compiled." Some of those changes end in a positive outcome, like developing opposable thumbs or intelligence, but some of them are not positive, and we characterize them as diseases.

The big problem with these diseases is the immense variability involved. Every human has 23 chromosomes with 21,000 genes and 3 billion base pairs that code who we are. With an average of 50,000 mutations in every human, finding the one responsible for a disease is like trying to find a needle in a haystack. That titanic work is now done manually. Depending on the symptoms, the potential mutations that could be causing the disease have to be filtered in a long process known as sequencing. Experience, knowledge, and even gut feeling are required to successfully diagnose the disease, in a process that can't scale and often relies on just luck.

When Julián learned all of that, he was determined to change it. He started small, getting together with a group of friends and coworkers, some of them with technical backgrounds. They developed a system to detect the mutations in more than 200 epilepsy genes, and they partnered with a local hospital in Spain to apply this technique to its patients. In just one year, the system was able to diagnose 1,400 patients suffering from Dravet syndrome and other genetic conditions.

That was the point of no return for Julián. He was now beyond determined to take this experiment to the next level and change the way rare diseases were diagnosed. In 2017 he founded a nonprofit organization to continue this work, together with some friends and acquaintances (I consider myself extremely lucky to be one of them). We all share the same passion for the mission, in most cases driven by similar personal circumstances in our families.

In this foundation, named Foundation 29 in honor of the International Day of Rare Diseases on February 29, Julián leads the application of AI techniques to advance medicine for rare diseases. One of the main projects is called Dx29, a tool designed to augment the capabilities of medical professionals and thereby speed up and increase the accuracy of diagnosis. The system is able to extract the patient's symptoms from their medical notes, match them with the DNA sequence of the patient, and identify potential candidates for the disease. It provides this list of candidates to the doctor, as well as proposing additional exploratory questions to narrow down the candidates until a diagnosis is correctly performed.

The early results of this approach are beyond anything Julián could have dreamed of when he started this journey. Initial tests performed with real doctors and patients have shown that diagnoses that often took months or even years in the past can now be made in days. In an iterative process, the doctor captures symptoms and interacts with the system to get additional clues and areas to explore. The doctor's capabilities are enhanced instead of replaced by the tool, which motivates them to embrace the technology instead of rejecting it.

Dx29 uses many of the AI capabilities you will see in the next chapter. First, a natural language processing model extracts symptoms from the patient's notes. To enable identification of the almost infinite ways of referring to symptoms and their variations, a word embedding technique is used, trained on 27 million medical publications. At runtime, the clinical notes are translated into English using neural translation and then processed by the symptoms extraction engine. A third AI model trained on a database of diseases and their associated genetic mutations is able to classify the mutations found in the sequencing by likelihood of being present, resulting in a list of top candidates to explore and key symptoms to check. The doctor can then explore those symptoms and refine the process iteratively until a diagnosis is found.

And Julián is not stopping here. He's optimistic that he can expand this technique to not only identify known rare diseases, but also classify previously undiscovered ones. The idea is based on the same concept as word embedding, but applied to the human genome. If we can map an individual genome to a mathematical vector that we can position in space, we could find new diseases that are close to existing diseases, helping us narrow the range of treatments to use and making the entire process much more effective than the blind approach used by doctors today with rare diseases that haven't been mapped to specific mutations.

All these AI capabilities are already well known in the technology industry, but it's when they're combined in a particular use case that the magic happens. In the next chapter, you will learn about these high-level capabilities so you can understand how to apply them to your specific scenario.

The AI Organization Defined

Thirty years ago, every business was looking at software as a way to redefine how it ran its operations. New *systems of record* were able to manage every core process in the enterprise, from accounting to payroll, resource planning, and customer management. This change was the foundation of the digital transformation—but as big a change as it was, the digitization of the core processes didn't alter the primary business of a company; it just made it more efficient.

In the past decade, however, systems of record have been extended with so-called *systems of engagement*. These systems redefine how companies engage with customers, how customers use and buy their products, and even what those products are. Along the way, software evolved from being focused on efficiencies to being a core aspect of business. Actually, it quickly became the part of business where the differentiation battle was fought. Companies using software cleverly were able to differentiate very quickly from more traditional companies: think Netflix, Airbnb, Uber, and Amazon. Even referring to these as media, real estate, transportation, and retail companies sounds weird; they are, in a sense, software companies, because they understand that software is a primary function inside the organization.

Modern companies look at software as something that is infused through every aspect of their business, a critical component of their operational efficiencies as well as their products and business models. Nowadays, every company is a software company.

The Emergence of AI

The full digitalization of companies has also had a secondary effect—the proliferation of data. Systems of record transformed what traditionally were paper files into digital stores containing all the business data behind the company's core processes. Systems of engagement added a vast amount of data about product usage and customer interactions. This created the perfect environment for the eruption of *systems of intelligence.*

Systems of intelligence leverage the vast amount of data generated in an enterprise to create expert systems. These systems are able to provide insights, optimize, and even predict future outcomes to help the business make better decisions. In the past decade, organizations all over the world began using techniques such as reporting, analytics, and data mining to create these systems of intelligence—but nobody was calling them artificial intelligence yet.

Traditionally the term *artificial intelligence* has been reserved for describing very special occasions when a machine has been able to perform tasks that are normally associated with human intelligence. As powerful as reporting or analytics can be, they're definitely not at that level. So, what happened? Why is everybody using the term AI now?

The primary reason for this change is the growing sophistication of the techniques available to build these systems, in particular in the area of machine learning. Machine learning techniques have been used in the past to build systems of intelligence. They can build a mathematical model based on sample data (also known as training data), which can make predictions without being explicitly programmed. This difference is illustrated in Figure 1-1.

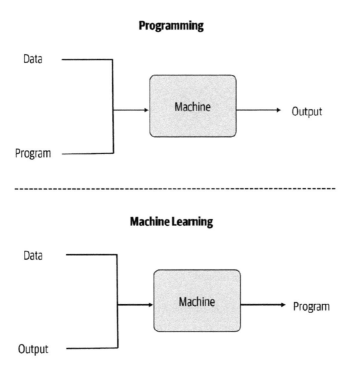

Figure 1-1. Programming versus machine learning

There are multiple algorithms that can be used for machine learning, but there's one in particular that is behind the explosion of use of the term AI: *artificial neural networks*.

Artificial neural networks are loosely based on how real neurons work in our brains, as shown in Figure 1-2. Each neuron is a simple activation function that is linked with other neurons via weighted connections. In recent years we've seen a huge amount of innovation related to this technique, with researchers creating more and more complex architectures of artificial neurons. This approach, with networks consisting of thousands of neurons and dozens of layers, is also referred to as *deep learning*.

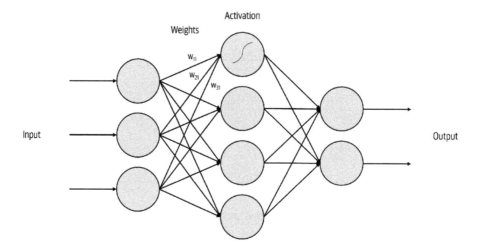

Figure 1-2. A simple artificial neural network

Deep learning is behind most of the AI breakthroughs reported increasingly frequently in the press. Using this technique, machines can now recognize objects in images, transcribe speech, answer questions about a text, or translate text from one language to another—all at a better rate of accuracy than a human can achieve, deserving without question the categorization of artificial intelligence. You will learn more about artificial neural networks and even create one yourself in Appendix A in this book.

AI Capabilities

Human intelligence is broad and complex. Some human achievements are definitely not in the realm of what machines can do now. It may be a long time before they get there, if they ever do. Abstract problem solving, concept generalization, emotional knowledge, creativity, and even self-awareness are all areas where even the most powerful deep learning algorithms cannot come close to human intelligence. The combination of all these cognitive abilities in a machine that can be generalized to any scenario is referred to as *artificial general intelligence*; for now, it's just a theoretical exercise.

However, current techniques are showing great success at performing narrower tasks traditionally reserved to human intelligence. We call this *narrow AI* or *weak AI*, and it refers primarily to three capabilities: learning, perception, and cognition.

LEARNING

The primary characteristic of machine learning is the ability to learn over time, without the need of explicit programming. Machine learning algorithms learn by exploring and doing, just like humans (though I'm sure those of you who are parents of young kids sometimes wish that wasn't the case!), and not by following a set of step-of-step instructions.

Machine learning algorithms are categorized depending on how they perform that learning. The most popular technique, and the one you will probably use 90% of the time in your enterprise, is *supervised learning*.

Supervised learning uses a set of data that contains both the input and the desired output. Through iterative optimization, the learning algorithm will find a function that can model how the inputs are transformed into the outputs. This model can then be applied to new inputs that are not part of the training set, predicting the associated outputs.

Finding the right algorithm and its parameters is part science, part creativity and gut feeling. How to apply machine learning to that process itself is a research topic of its own—the technique is called *automated machine learning* (*https://oreil.ly/AIO_1-1*), or AutoML. If you want to experiment with machine learning and learn more about it, check out the "AI crash course" in Appendix A.

Supervised algorithms all have the same flaw: they require a lot of data. And not just any kind of data; they require training data that includes both the inputs and the associated outputs, also referred to as *labeled data.*

Sometimes we will have historical data stored by our systems of record or systems of engagement that is already labeled. Think, for example, of a customer churn model—we can look at our historical data on customers who have churned and use that as the output for the training data in addition to the customers' history of interactions. Using the right algorithm, we will be able to predict customer churn in the future just by looking at a new set of interactions.

Sometimes, however, we won't be that lucky, and the data won't be labeled. *Unsupervised algorithms* take a set of unlabeled data and find structure in it. *Clustering* is the most popular type of unsupervised algorithm: it uses different techniques to find groups in data based on commonalities. You may use these algorithms for identifying customer segments in your customer base or among your website visitors. Other commonly used unsupervised techniques are association rules (which can identify associations in the data, such as people who bought a particular product being interested in others) and anomaly detection (finding rare or suspicious elements that differ from the majority of data).

In other cases, we don't use any training data at all. Think of how humans learn to play a video game. A supervised approach to this problem would be to watch thousands of games to learn from them. That's the business model for many YouTubers that my kids watch, but I find that approach tremendously boring. A more interesting way to learn is to actually play the game. As we play, we get positive reinforcement when we do something well (e.g., we get points) and negative reinforcement when we do something wrong (e.g., we get killed). *Reinforcement learning* algorithms do exactly that: they learn the machine learning function by exploring the environment and reinforcing the right behavior.

Reinforcement learning is an amazingly promising area of machine learning in business because of its data-less nature. It is especially suited to autonomous systems—both mobile, such as cars or drones, and static, such as HVAC or power systems—but it can also be used for complex business processes. Reinforcement learning is usually identified as the most difficult discipline in AI, but the crash course in Appendix A will teach you the basic concepts and even how to create your first reinforcement learning algorithm.

PERCEPTION

If there's one area that has traditionally been exclusive to humans, it is *perception*. For decades we've been trying to mimic humankind's ability to perceive the world around us, with limited success. The complexity of understanding an image or converting speech to text made it extremely difficult for this to be done programmatically—just imagine defining the step-by-step instructions required to identify a horse in a picture!

Machine learning algorithms are a much better fit for this kind of problem. However, the accuracy of traditional machine learning algorithms when applied to perception tasks hasn't even come close to what a human can achieve. (I still remember demoing the speech recognition feature in Windows Vista for developers...it definitely made me a stronger person!)

Take image classification, for example. The ImageNet challenge (*https://oreil.ly/AIO_1-2*) is the most popular challenge for image classification. Since 2010, participants all over the world have submitted their algorithms in a race to build the most accurate model. At the beginning of the competition, in 2010, a good error rate was around 25%. For comparison, the human equivalent error rate on the same dataset is around 5.1%. In 2012 Alex Krizhevsky, a student at the University of Toronto, submitted as his solution a neural network consisting of eight layers called AlexNet (*https://oreil.ly/AIO_1-3*). It crushed the competition, achieving an error rate of 15.3%—10 points lower than the next contender.

During the following years the technique he introduced was improved and more layers were added, with GoogLeNet, a 22-layer neural network, achieving an error rate of 6.7% in 2014. The following year, a team at Microsoft Research submitted an entry that used a new neural network technique: its residual neural net (*https://oreil.ly/AIO_1-4*), which had a depth of a whopping 152 layers, achieved an error rate of only 3.57%, surpassing human performance for the first time.

Deep learning changed computer vision forever. Today, this technique is used for virtually every scenario in computer vision with high accuracy, making it one of the most popular use cases in the enterprise. Here are some examples of tasks that computer vision is used for today:

- Classify the content of an image (image classification)
- Recognize multiple objects in an image, and identify the bounds for each (object detection)
- Recognize scenes or activities in images (e.g., unsafe situations in the workplace, or restocking needs in retail stores)
- Detect faces, recognize them, and even identify emotions for each
- Recognize written text, including handwritten text (optical character recognition)
- Identify offensive content in images and videos

In their book *Telling Ain't Training* (ASTD Press), researchers Harold Stolovitch and Erica Keeps assert that 83% of the information we receive comes from our sense of sight. Hearing is next, providing 11% of our sensory input; together, the two account for 94% of all the information we receive from the external world. There's no doubt that audio processing is the other big area of focus for AI, right after computer vision.

Similar deep learning techniques can be applied to audio signals, helping computers identify sounds. You can use this ability to identify birds by their songs, or predict failures in wind turbines by the sounds they make.

But the most exciting use of AI in audio processing is definitely speech recognition. The reference dataset used for speech recognition is called Switchboard: it contains approximately 260 hours of two-sided telephone conversations. The measured transcription error rate for humans is 5.9%; it was equaled by a neural network designed by Microsoft Research in 2016 and beaten a year later with a 5.1% error rate (*https://oreil.ly/AIO_1-5*). For the first time, a machine was able to understand humans better than humans themselves.

These breakthroughs are not only enabling machines to understand us, but also to communicate back to us in natural ways. In 2018 the text-to-speech service (*https://oreil.ly/AIO_1-6*) available in Azure, also developed with deep learning techniques, was able to synthesize human voice at a level of quality virtually undistinguishable from a real one.

The conjunction of these capabilities can also enable the holy grail of computer science: fully natural user interfaces (NUIs). With machines that can not only see and understand humans, but can communicate back to us using natural speech, it seems we've accomplished the dream of every sci-fi movie ever. Have we really, though? To truly have a meaningful interaction with a computer, it should not only be able to transcribe what we say, but also understand the meaning of speech.

Natural language processing (NLP) is the field of AI that analyzes, understands, and derives meaning from human language. One of the most common scenarios for NLP is language understanding, the foundation for modern conversational AI experiences such as digital assistants. When you ask Siri, Alexa, or Cortana about the weather, the system first transforms your speech audio into text, then applies a natural language understanding model to extract your intent. The intent (e.g., "get weather") is then mapped to an output (in this case, providing information on the local weather).

NLP techniques have exploded in the past few years. Some of them are useful only for basic tasks such as sentiment analysis, keyword extraction, or entity identification, but others can be used for more complex tasks like text summarization or translation. In 2018, the machine translation team at Microsoft was able to achieve human parity on automatic translation (*https://oreil.ly/AIO_1-7*)—an extremely complex task, and a goal previously considered unachievable—for the first time.

One of the most exciting uses of natural language understanding is machine reading comprehension. In January 2018, a team at Microsoft Research Asia was able to achieve human parity using the Stanford Question Answering Dataset (SQuAD), a machine reading dataset that is made up of questions about a set of Wikipedia articles. In fact, the system was able to perform better than a human (*https://oreil.ly/AIO_1-8*) at providing answers to open questions related to those articles. Many companies have continued to contribute to this challenge (*https://oreil.ly/AIO_1-9*), taking it even further.

Still, these systems don't use the same level of abstraction as humans. At its core, a question-answering algorithm will search the text for clues that can point to the right answer. For every question, the system will search the entire text for a match. Humans do that too (especially if we are in a hurry), but when we truly want to understand a piece of text we extract knowledge from it, to generalize it and make it more consumable.

Imagine a text describing the state of California. Humans would generalize the entity "California" from that text and add attributes to it (e.g., population, size), and even relationships with other entities (e.g., neighbor states, governor). After that generalization, we don't need the text any more to answer questions about California; we have generalized the knowledge about it.

The equivalent in artificial intelligence for this process is called *knowledge extraction*, and it has profound implications in the enterprise. Using these techniques, we can extract high-level concepts from chaotic, unstructured, and even confusing information. The resulting knowledge graph can be used not only to answer broad-ranging questions across our entire data estate, but also to navigate and understand that information.

That level of abstraction goes way beyond the traditional capabilities of NLP, taking it closer to what we know as cognition.

COGNITION

Strictly speaking, *cognition* is the ability to acquire and process knowledge. It involves high-level constructs that our minds use for reasoning, understanding, problem solving, planning, and decision making.

The techniques we have explored so far involve some level of cognition, although it is not always apparent. Take image classification as an example. If we closely examine a deep neural network used for image classification, we can actually see how the neural network is decomposing the problem into smaller steps in every layer. Without human intervention, the neural network automatically shows some level of generalization: the first layers detect simple characteristics such as edges or textures. As we get deeper into the neural network, layers are able to extract more complex features such as patterns or elements. In a sense, the neural network has been able to acquire some knowledge and do some basic reasoning with it.

Natural language processing shows similar intrinsic abstractions. At their core, most modern NLP techniques use a concept called *word embedding*. With word embedding, every word in a text is transformed into a vector that represents the meaning of the word. In this new space, words that are semantically similar (for example, "weather" and "forecast") are closer to each other. Using that approach, the system will match the sentences "What's the weather today?" and "Get the forecast for the next 24 hours" to the same intent. Even if the words are different, their embeddings are similar because they are semantically close to each other. Translation works the same way: translation techniques use word embeddings to abstract the input text and turn it into a language-independent "idea" that can then be translated into any language using the reverse process.

In all these cases, cognition is intrinsic to the perception. However, many AI scenarios are purely cognitive. They are not focused on perceiving the world around us, but rather aim to abstract it and reason on top of that abstraction. Some of the most foundational supervised learning approaches are like that. *Regression* is the ability to predict a numerical value based on some available information; for example, estimating a house's value based on its features and location, or forecasting sales based on historical data. *Classification* is the ability to identify the class or category of an item based on its features; for example, identifying whether or not a house is likely to be sold to a particular buyer. *Optimization* algorithms reason on top of a process to maximize a particular outcome, like allocating the resources in a hospital.

Recommendation systems are able to find similarities between items like movies, books, or songs not apparent to humans, just by looking at ratings or purchasing behavior. Other techniques, like clustering, can find patterns in data and group items in an unsupervised way, as mentioned earlier.

We see the same cognition capabilities in reinforcement learning techniques as well. In 2017, the Microsoft Research Lab in Montreal (previously Maluba) was able to set a new record for Ms. Pac-Man (*https://oreil.ly/AIO_1-10*), crossing the one million point barrier for the first time. The system was trained by playing thousands of games by itself. Similarly, OpenAI Five—a team of five neural networks—began to beat human teams at Dota 2 (*https://oreil.ly/AIO_1-11*) in 2018; OpenAI Five was trained by playing 180 years' worth of games against itself every day. The most famous example is probably the accomplishment achieved by Google DeepMind: its system, AlphaGo (*https://oreil.ly/AIO_1-12*), was the first to be able to beat a 9-dan professional player of Go, a game that is considered much more difficult for computers than others, like chess. Closely watching games played by any of these AI systems will give you the impression that they're exhibiting another characteristic of cognition—*planning*. The system is able to "think" in advance what the best approach is to maximize its score in the long term.

AI Capabilities Cheat Sheet

Since I moved to the United States 10 years ago, every year in the summer I've gone back to Spain with my family for a vacation. The trip from Redmond, WA, to my hometown in Cádiz takes about 24 hours, with three different flights. As any parent with three kids will know, there's a question you will hear approximately a million times in such a journey (the first time probably just as you're leaving your house, on the way to the airport): *Are we there yet?*

I have a similar feeling when it comes to AI. For the past few years, customers have been asking "Are we there yet?" In a world of AI over-hype, it's difficult to separate reality from fiction, and true capabilities from marketing stunts.

The good news is that *we are there*. AI is real today, and thousands of companies are using it to transform their business. You should definitely be conscious of the future possibilities of AI, but it's more important that you understand what AI can do *today*.

The following cheat sheet (Figure 1-3) can be handy for that purpose: it provides a summary of the core capabilities introduced in this chapter. All of them are real today and we will use them extensively in the rest of the book, applying them to real business scenarios.

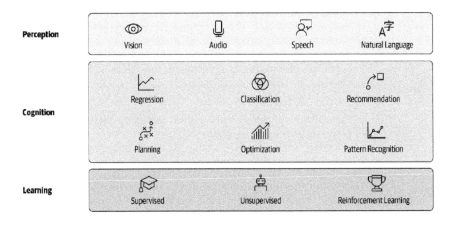

Figure 1-3. The AI capabilities cheat sheet

Tables 1-1 through 1-3 provide additional information about each of these core capabilities.

Table 1-1. Perception—interpreting the world around us

AI capability	Use case
Vision	Extract information from or understand images and videos—for example, performing image classification, scene identification, or face recognition.
Audio	Perform audio processing tasks such as sound recognition or audio pattern identification—for example, identifying machinery failures based on sound.
Speech	Interact with humans using speech—for example, performing natural text-to-speech and speech-to-text conversions.
Natural Language	Understand and generate text language—for example, identifying intent, extracting concepts, analyzing sentiment, or answering questions.

Table 1-2. Cognition—reasoning on top of data

AI capability	Use case
Regression	Estimate a numerical value based on other variables or their values over time—for example, predicting house values or forecasting sales.
Classification	Identify a set of categories of a given instance—for example, fraud detection or medical diagnosis.
Recommendation	Predict a user's preference for a particular item given similarities with other items or other users' preferences—for example, movie recommendations or experience personalization.
Planning	Find the best sequential approach for a goal—for example, identifying a path for an autonomous vehicle or the steps in a business process.

AI capability	Use case
Optimization	Maximize a given outcome by finding the right parameters in a process—for example, resource allocation or dynamic pricing.
Pattern Recognition	Augment the decision-making process by providing relevant insights on data—for example, clustering or key factor identification.

Table 1-3. Learning—learning without being explicitly programmed

AI capability	Use case
Supervised	Learn by iterating over training datasets containing labeled data (pairs of inputs and outputs)—for example, using data on previous customer interactions to predict churn.
Unsupervised	Infer hidden structures in an unlabeled dataset, such as relationships, categories, patterns, or features—for example, identifying different usage patterns or user segments in a website.
Reinforcement Learning	Learn by experimenting in an environment, trying to maximize a reward provided in the training—for example, operating a vehicle autonomously or optimizing the energy consumption in a datacenter.

The AI Organization

The addition of these new capabilities represents a profound transformation in software—and therefore business—as we know it. AI changes the way software is created, from providing step-by-step instructions to learning through data and experiences. It enables new ways for machines to interact with users and the world around them, through perception and natural interfaces, and cognitive capabilities make it possible to reason on top of the acquired information.

Think of every other evolution of software in the past three decades. The client/server paradigm born with the PC radically transformed the software experience in the enterprise. The internet, which one can argue represented a change in how software is consumed and distributed, caused a technology disruption that affected every industry. Mobile computing created entire new customer engagements and business models.

All these disruptions may pale in comparison with AI. Learning, perception, and cognition provide a whole new toolbox that will enable a new generation of software. And with every company being a software company nowadays, a new generation of software also means a new generation of companies. I like to refer to that new breed of companies as *AI organizations*.

Just like the transition to software companies, the transition to AI organizations involves a left-to-right rethinking of how organizations run their operations, engage their customers, empower their employees, and even define their products. Each function in the organization can be redefined with the new AI toolbox.

That makes starting difficult. With so many new tools and so many use cases to apply them, where do we begin? Business leaders often ask about the typical use cases of AI. The approach in many organizations is to identify as many use cases as possible, prioritize them with the framework of their choice, and execute a few, hoping some of them will achieve promising results.

Instead, I prefer to think of the AI transformation as a journey. Each tactical use case that I execute is a step that's part of a broader strategy. The culmination of that strategy is to redefine the entire organization with AI.

You can visualize the stages in this journey as a set of concentric circles, as shown in Figure 1-4. At the core are the technical departments in your organization, where the transformation usually begins. This may be your IT department, or your Development department, or a distributed function in your organization that has been on point for your software transformation over the past years. In the next ring are your business units. These are the different areas in your organization that represent business functions beyond technology: both horizontal business units (sales, marketing, finance, HR) and vertical business units specific to your industry. The last ring contains the employees in the organization—those supporting the business (back office employees) and those directly involved with the production and customer engagement (front-line employees).

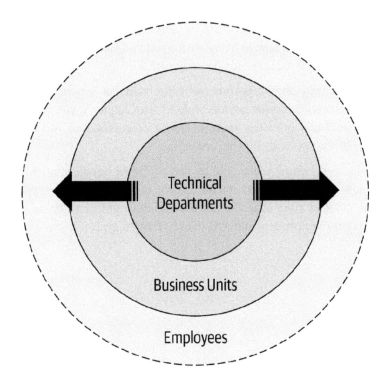

Figure 1-4. The journey of an AI organization

These rings are interconnected. You cannot transform your business units without a transformation in your technical departments. You cannot expect every employee to use AI if the business units have not embraced it. In a sense, these concentric rings are similar to a platform stack: instead of isolated use cases, the AI organization has a comprehensive approach to AI in which the layers build on top of one another.

In the next three chapters, we cover what it means to transform each of these rings. You will see how to apply the learning, perception, and cognition capabilities discussed here to each of the rings, identifying the use cases that will help you get started. You will also learn how to evaluate different use cases, not only in terms of their direct results but also their overall impact and contribution to the AI organization journey.

At the end of this journey, AI should be a primary component of your organization and not just an ingredient for isolated use cases:

- AI should be a first-class citizen in your technical departments. In Chapter 2, you will see how to bring AI into all your software applications and create new ones that are only possible with AI.

- Business units should partner with the technical departments to jointly redefine every business process with AI. In Chapter 3, you will learn how to identify and prioritize these business processes, and you will explore many of the use cases for your industry.

- Finally, every employee should be part of the AI transformation. In Chapter 4, you will see how to ensure that the technical departments and business units in your organization provide the right platform to effectively empower employees to apply AI to everything they do.

AI Hero: Kriti

Kriti (*https://oreil.ly/AIO_2a-1*) grew up in the state of Rajasthan, in northern India. She had a happy childhood with supportive parents who encouraged her to learn and be independent. But even with that kind of encouragement, nobody would have guessed then that Kriti was going to be recognized later in her life as one of the 30 under 30 by Forbes for advancements in AI.

Like many other AI heroes you will get to know in this book, Kriti's attitude toward her constraints defined her. She didn't have access to a computer or the internet beyond the 10 computers available in her school for thousands of students, but she did have access to the library, which opened up an entire world of knowledge for her. At the age of 12 she built her own computer, putting together different parts she'd acquired for a few dollars.

When she was still a teenager, she was invited to visit a government space research lab. Kriti was fascinated by space exploration and how computers can help us analyze the huge amount of data gathered about the universe to understand it better. But that wasn't what captured her imagination the most: it was how a particular researcher was using one of the computers that changed her life. Instead of a keyboard or mouse, this researcher was using voice commands to control their computer. From that moment, she knew she wanted one of those computers (at that time the size of a room!) for herself.

It was the same independent streak and desire to learn that took her to university—a remarkable occurrence, as most of Kriti's peers instead were destined for marriage at a young age. The median age at first marriage for women in India is 16.4 years (*https://oreil.ly/AIO_2a-2*), and in some areas female literacy is as low as 50%. Those numbers, among others, would come back to haunt Kriti years after she left India.

After graduating from the University of Rajasthan, she received a full scholarship to the University of St. Andrews in Scotland, where she obtained a master's degree in advanced computer science. She was about to accept another full scholarship for a PhD in Oxford when she realized she couldn't wait any longer—it was time to stop studying and start applying AI in the real world.

Kriti's first job was at Barclays. Like many other industries, banking has experienced a huge transformation driven by technology and software. Kriti's role was to transform the bank once again, this time to make it a data company. As you'll learn in the next chapter, that transformation can start by focusing on existing business applications and how to make them better with AI. For example, Kriti's team modernized the existing rules-based applications for financial transactions and applied modern AI-driven techniques instead, dramatically improving the customer experience.

In her next job, Kriti concentrated on conversational AI. Technology that had once only been available at research institutions like the one she'd visited as a schoolgirl was now available to any computer or smartphone user. She was fascinated by how natural conversational interfaces can make technology more accessible and easier to use; that's not only cool, but also has profound implications for the democratization of technology. Instead of humans learning how to communicate with computers, computers can learn how to communicate with us.

Kriti joined Sage, one of the largest business applications companies in the world, to pursue that goal. Sage's main customers are not big corporations with ranks of accountants and tax experts. Most of their customers are small businesses that struggle to keep up with the administrative work. They spend an average of 120 days a year on administrative tasks, which takes a huge toll on their productivity and stops them from being proactive and forward-looking, limiting growth in what is the backbone of many economies in the world.

As Sage's VP of AI, Kriti began working to change that. In 2016 she helped create Pegg, one of the first business-oriented conversational AI agents in the market. Pegg was intended to help small companies manage their finances through a chat-based interface available in popular messaging apps like Slack, Skype, and Facebook Messenger. It makes administrative tasks such as uploading a receipt, logging a payment, or checking a balance as simple as texting a friend. On the backend, Pegg uses AI to help business owners without accounting experience to be proactive with their finances. It can make recommendations, send notifications for accounts about to go past due, and provide future projections.

Pegg is a great example of how AI can democratize technology to underserved audiences—in this case, small businesses. But this was just the beginning for Kriti. Her next project, leveraging the same technologies she was using to transform corporations, would be motivated by her memories of her childhood in India.

Growing up in India as a woman was very different from Kriti's new life in London. India is considered to be the world's most dangerous country (*https:// oreil.ly/AIO_2a-3*) for sexual violence against women. A crime against a woman is committed in India every 3 minutes (*https://oreil.ly/AIO_2a-4*), and every 20 minutes a woman is raped. The problem is deeply rooted in society. A staggering 65% of Indian men (*https://oreil.ly/AIO_2a-5*) believe women should tolerate violence and that they sometimes deserve to be beaten. Some 24% of men also admit they have committed sexual violence at some point during their lives.

In such an environment, it's not difficult to imagine the constant fear that many parents of girls in India suffer. Kriti still remembers how her parents wouldn't let her go outside by herself. She was lucky, though: some Indian parents do not even want a daughter in the first place. Selective abortions and even female infanticide are the most horrible consequences of gender inequality: in Rajasthan, the state where Kriti grew up, there are 888 girls for every 1,000 boys (*https://oreil.ly/AIO_2a-6*) under the age of 6.

It was during a dinner with a group of women in South Africa when that reality came back to Kriti's mind. It was a regular dinner, but the casual nature of it added a halo of safety that led one of the women to share about suffering domestic violence at home. Suddenly, more of the women around the table began sharing their experiences. Most of them had suffered at least one episode of sexual, physical, or psychological abuse.

Kriti was shocked by these stories, but unfortunately the chances of finding several women with past experiences of abuse in South Africa are quite high. One in three women face physical, sexual, or psychological violence at home. In most cases, the violence stays within those walls; only 5% to 10% of such incidents are ever reported, and when they are, it's usually too late. The average number of episodes of abuse a woman suffers before asking the authorities for help is 35. The first 34 times she keeps silent, often because of the social stigma or just shame of admitting having been abused by her own partner.

Kriti was not an expert in such a difficult problem, nor did she think she could fix it completely. But she knew technology could help. Working with local institutions, she created rAInbow, a digital companion for women at risk of abuse. Research and interviews with abuse victims have shown that rAInbow is able to help women in toxic relationships realize they are being abused and take action. Not having a real person on the other side actually makes the system more approachable: conversations with rAInbow are nonjudgmental and unbiased as well as emotionally aware.

Just as Pegg has an AI backend that can provide proactive insights about finance, rAInbow can identify early signs of abuse and be proactive. It has been trained to recognize behavior patterns leading to abuse, inform victims of their rights, and encourage them to seek assistance.

rAInbow was launched in 2018 in partnership with Nelson Mandela's step-daughter Josina Machel, who had also lived through a horrific domestic violence experience that left her blind in one eye. Since then, hundreds of thousands of women have used the service, and it has made a huge difference in many of their lives. rAInbow was recently recognized as one of the top digital innovations of the year by UNESCO.

After working on rAInbow, Kriti kept identifying social issues that could be addressed with technology. She didn't have to search far, as things in her native hometown had not changed much since she'd left. Gender disparity is deeply rooted in Indian society, and from early childhood women are raised in a culture in which information is withheld by adults. Sex education is a taboo, and girls often have to face their sexual maturity without any help: 9 out of 10 girls in India don't know what their period is, and many think they are dying when it first happens to them. They don't have any information on birth control and they are not aware of the risks of sexually transmitted diseases.

With the help of the Population Foundation of India, Kriti launched another digital assistant called Dr. Sneha in early 2019. Like rAInbow, Dr. Sneha is a friendly digital companion with whom users can have unbiased, nonjudgmental conversations; girls can feel safe asking Dr. Sneha the questions they cannot ask the adults around them. The service can be used even on very low-cost phones, and it is distributed through community centers in rural areas where girls don't have access to mobile devices. The interface is also adapted for the low literacy rates still present in some of those areas, using visual cues and video storytelling instead of plain text. In its first month, it had already provided one million sexual-health consultations to young people in India.

As I was writing this book, Kriti had just left her leadership position at Sage to fully dedicate her career to the use of AI for social issues at AI for Good, an organization she founded with the mission of creating technologies for solving some of the toughest challenges facing humanity. In speaking to her, you can feel Kriti's excitement for the journey ahead. But that excitement has little to do with creating new breakthroughs in technology, or advancements in AI. Actually, some of Kriti's biggest accomplishments didn't use the most complex or cutting-edge AI techniques; she just used core AI technologies to create better software (which you will learn to do in the next chapter). Her excitement comes from applying this new breed of software to real problems. It comes from combining the scale of software with the human-centric possibilities of AI to create products that can help millions of abuse victims to open up and look for help, or girls to learn about sexual and reproductive health.

The world of the future will need AI leaders like Kriti. More than ever, technology will need to be more human, and the people behind it will need to recognize that.

## 2

The Technical Transformation: Bringing AI to Every Application

You'll often hear that technology and business have to come together in an organization in order for it to successfully embrace AI. You will see this in Chapter 3, as well as strategies to make it happen—but it doesn't have to start out that way. Just like Kriti's beginnings at Barclays or Sage, the journey to the AI organization can start with a purely technical approach. This first step—transforming your technical departments—is the focus of this chapter.

At the end of the day, you can consider AI as *better software*. As long as you continue the journey, starting with the technical aspects will give you a strong foundation to build on and help you quickly differentiate yourself from your competitors.

Starting on the technical side will also help you build the necessary AI muscle to address the broader AI transformation. The scarcity of AI technical talent is one of the most important blockers for AI adoption in the enterprise, but exposing your technical teams to real AI projects will encourage reskilling and talent acquisition. This will need to be associated with a corresponding training initiative (more on this in Chapter 8), and it will allow you to leverage the existing software muscle in your organization.

Understanding Your Application Portfolio

Identifying the list of software candidates to transform is relatively simple. You don't need to inventory assets that are traditionally not well documented in the enterprise, such as the data estate or the business processes. Your list of candidates is simply your application portfolio, a usually well-identified and well-documented source.

There are several frameworks for modeling this application portfolio. They all have differences in terminology, but at their core they all identify different types of applications depending on their pace of change and user experience. The two main application types are *systems of record* (SoRs) and *systems of engagement* (SoEs):

- SoRs are applications that are running core aspects of the business, don't change much over time, and are focused on effectiveness and optimization.

- SoEs are applications that are providing the primary interfaces for the business, are in continuous evolution, and are focused on user and employee engagement.

This classification is extremely useful for managing the application portfolio in your organization. Trying to run both types of applications with the same approach is a bad idea. They are optimized for different things, and as such, they need different processes and will evolve at different speeds.

Understanding how your organization is currently managing its application portfolio is relevant for your AI modernization strategy. Systems of record such as customer relationship management (CRM) systems, enterprise resource planning (ERP) systems, and supply chain management (SCM) systems are usually outsourced with out-of-the-box solutions or sprawling customizations that are difficult to manage and evolve, but they provide a very strong and stable foundation. On the other hand, some organizations look at these systems as a core aspect of their business and decide to create and maintain them by themselves with their own custom solutions.

Systems of engagement are usually a mix of in-house, outsourced, and out-of-the-box solutions, but they tend to be much easier to evolve. They are more likely to follow modern software architectures that focus on independent micro-apps for user engagement (e.g., websites, mobile apps) and independent microservices (*https://oreil.ly/AIO_2-1*) for the backend (e.g., REST services, containers).

This taxonomy is always evolving. There's a clear trend in the industry to move more and more applications to the SoE model, as these are much easier to evolve and innovate with. However, those migration projects are hugely expensive and difficult to justify with short-term returns on investment. The typical reality is a mix: companies usually maintain these monolithic and stable systems of record but make them more accessible to modern applications through APIs as they gradually modernize them. For example, it is very common for a bank to run on a monolithic system of record (the core banking system) that is exposed through APIs to the modern systems of engagement (website, mobile app, etc.).

Approaches to Software Transformation with AI

Why is it so important to understand the different application types in your application portfolio? Because AI is not a mature discipline. It requires experimentation, quick iterations of trial and error, and because of the way it is developed it learns over time. Trying to fit AI into the rigorous processes of systems of record can result in a huge mismatch, and probably a scar for life on your organization.

When identifying use cases for software modernization with AI, focus on the more agile and flexible systems of engagement. Even if you think an existing system of record can benefit from AI, resist the temptation to infuse AI into it. Just like banks didn't add websites or mobile apps to their core banking code in Cobol, it is a good idea to implement AI as a separate system of engagement that interacts with the rest of the system through an API.

Once you do that, you can think about how you might apply the core capabilities of AI (learning, perception, and cognition) to your application portfolio and identify the use cases most relevant for your business. There are two approaches that you can take:

- Infusing AI into your applications, making them more engaging and productive

- Creating new applications only possible with AI, with conversational AI interfaces

Infusing AI into Your Applications

Applications that are part of your systems of engagement usually have two primary goals:

- For your customer-facing applications, the primary success metrics are usually related to engagement: number of active users, time spent, customer activation, conversion to sales, etc.

- For your employee-facing applications, the primary success metrics are usually related to productivity: time saved, tasks performed, escalation rate, etc.

AI can greatly help with both, and cloud providers like Microsoft Azure, Google Cloud, or Amazon Web Services offer prebuilt, customizable AI services that can make the process of infusing AI into applications relatively easy (you can learn how to use one of these services in the crash course in Appendix A).

Where to do this will depend entirely on your business. A good rule of thumb is to start with the applications that are the most relevant to your business. For heavily customer-facing organizations the pick is usually obvious: Uber would pick its primary customer-facing mobile app, Walmart would pick its online store, Telefónica would pick its landline device. For less customer-facing organizations, the first picks are usually apps employees spend a lot of time using.

In general, the selection criteria should include factors like these:

- How relevant is the application to the business?

- Do we have full control of the application? In other words, is it fully owned by the organization or does it rely on third parties?

- What's the expected impact of infusing AI? That is, what engagement/productivity metric do we think it will impact, and how much?

- How much effort and time will be required? For example, is the service available as a prebuilt offering? If not, does the organization have the data and expertise to build it?

- Will it differentiate our organization in the market? If so, is that differentiation sustainable or does it have low entry barriers?

- Will this application benefit from network effects? For example, will infusing AI create a virtuous cycle, such as more data creating better AI, attracting more customers, and creating more data?

Once you've selected your target applications, AI has a huge span of capabilities to offer. A good approach is to start with the goal in mind, and think about which AI capabilities can help you achieve that goal. Is your goal to create a more engaging application, or do you want to increase user productivity? AI can offer huge opportunities for both.

CREATING MORE ENGAGING APPLICATIONS

If there's one area commonly identified with AI, it is its ability to enable more engaging applications. Actually, one of the canonical examples of AI is directly targeted at increasing the time spent in the application—the *recommender system*.

Automatic recommendations are not new. We've been creating recommenders for years with traditional programming techniques, statistics, traditional machine learning algorithms, and more recently, deep learning. At every step the relevance and accuracy of these recommenders have been improving, and therefore their business impact has been growing. About 75% of viewer activity on Netflix (*https://oreil.ly/AIO_2-2*) is driven by its famous recommender system, and 35% of what consumers purchase on Amazon (*https://oreil.ly/AIO_2-3*) comes from product recommendations based on these algorithms.

At their core, these recommender systems are very similar. They rely on collaborative filtering techniques: the items recommended to a user are based on the preferences of similar users, who are clustered based on their preferences. The preferences might be explicit (such as ratings or likes), or they could be based on subtler implicit signals, such as visits to a product page, time spent on the page, search queries, etc. The possibilities are almost infinite, and the impact follows the Pareto principle—if you are not using recommendations today in your systems of engagement, you can easily get 80% of the benefit with a 20% effort.

Recommender systems are data-hungry, though. You will need an existing dataset of customer behavior to make the system relevant, which can be tricky, especially for long-tail cases like products that are not sold very often or movies that are not watched much. Some techniques can be used to avoid that shortcoming; actually, most recommender systems nowadays use a hybrid approach of collaborative filtering and content-based systems. With the latter, you classify your items statically (e.g., by gender, category, or type) and recommend items with similar attributes. For example, if the user likes horror movies (which wouldn't be me, certainly!), you'll show them other movies in the horror genre. This attribute extraction can be powered by AI as well. For example, Bing Ads uses computer vision to extract text and other information from advertisements in order to increase the applicability of the ads it displays to the search query performed by the user. Reuters automatically embeds videos in news articles (*https://oreil.ly/AIO_2-4*) by extracting the topics covered in the article with AI.

Another popular way to increase user engagement is *personalization*. Traditionally, application and web development relied on A/B testing techniques to optimize the user experience: a developer could create two different versions of the interface and release them simultaneously to different sets of users, and after a period of time, they could look at the engagement metrics to decide which user experience was more engaging.

AI can scale that process to the point that the interface is optimized individually: you can present slightly different experiences to users, and based on their behavior you can optimize the experience for each of them. The home screen in Xbox uses this approach. The system uses a reinforcement learning algorithm to optimize what tiles to show and in what order, based on what tiles a user has clicked in the past and what other users are clicking.

Machine learning techniques can also be applied to other user actions. Using the historical data on click-through for the notifications raised by your application, you can optimize what to show and when to show these notifications to increase their effectiveness. Windows 10 uses this technique to decide when to show system notifications or tips.

Other uses of AI are not directly connected to user engagement but can help in the long term. For example, it can be used to:

- Increase the security of an application, making users more likely to trust it and engage more often with it. For example, Uber (*https://oreil.ly/AIO_2-5*) uses computer vision as an authentication factor for the driver, increasing security for passengers.

- Scale the analysis of feedback coming from the user, with techniques like sentiment analysis or entity extraction. For example, travel agencies can use AI to analyze hotel user reviews and identify issues in real time. Geocaching (*https://oreil.ly/AIO_2-6*), an entertainment company that provides an outdoor treasure hunting experience, uses sentiment analysis and key phrase extraction from its comment logs to uncover valuable insights and resolve issues quickly.

AI opens up new ways of interacting that can make our applications more engaging or accessible to more users. Today, prebuilt AI services can help us create systems that use text in multiple languages, human voice, gestures, ink, or even eye movement as the user input. You can use these techniques to make your existing applications more accessible and attractive to a broader set of users, but you can also use them to create entirely new form factors for your business, like retail kiosks, bank concierges, no-screen applications, and more. Equadex is a French company that commercializes the app Helpicto (*https://oreil.ly/ AIO_2-7*), a good example of an app that uses a natural interface to make it more engaging. Helpicto uses voice and pictograms to help people on the autism spectrum to communicate.

Augmented reality also makes heavy use of AI techniques, to perceive the world around the user and augment it. These augmented experiences represent a whole new level of user engagement and can be used in scenarios such as remote assistance, training, augmented processes, and many others. Chevron, for example, uses HoloLens (*https://oreil.ly/AIO_2-8*) to enable its refinery operators with remote expert assistance powered by augmented reality. The Oslo University Hospital is currently testing augment reality for a HoloLens-based surgery augmentation system (*https://oreil.ly/AIO_2-9*), providing surgeons with a roadmap to successfully navigate around internal organs.

CREATING MORE PRODUCTIVE APPLICATIONS

Funnily enough, in many situations your goal is not to increase the time spent on your systems of engagement, but to reduce it. Another set of AI uses cases are aimed at reducing the time needed by the user to perform their tasks. These techniques are especially relevant for applications that represent a time-consuming activity in your organization, and can be a great source of cost savings in the short term.

Data entry is definitely a time-consuming activity in most internal applications. AI techniques like computer vision and optical character recognition (OCR) in particular can simplify the process dramatically. Form-based OCR is a mature use case of AI that can be applied to existing applications, such as bank forms or expense reports—for example, the Danish accounting specialist Dinero (*https://oreil.ly/AIO_2-10*) automates the submission of invoices for its customers by automatically extracting the key elements with OCR. Less obvious scenarios are also providing very promising results. For example, object detection can be used to accelerate data entry: car insurance claims, urban damage notifications, and equipment ordering can be greatly simplified by extracting data automatically from images.

In other scenarios, data has to be entered manually. In those cases, smart autocompletion powered by AI can accelerate the process: based on existing information and contextual information, the system can recommend potential content for the form automatically. For example, Outlook replaced its autocompletion system for contacts and search with an AI-powered algorithm that makes the autocompletion much more relevant to users. In an extreme application of this concept, Outlook, LinkedIn, and Gmail are also able to recommend several full answers to an incoming email based on the its content, learning from past messages. For developers, Visual Studio is able to provide automatic completion in your source code, learning from the code of millions of other developers on GitHub.

For tasks that are more creative, AI can assist the user and provide support in the creation process. PowerPoint, for example, provides design ideas based on the current content in a slide, and hints on how to become a better presenter by listening to your rehearsal. Excel can provide ideas to help you better understand your data by automatically identifying patterns.

Search is another common capability in systems of engagement that can be significantly improved with AI, reducing the time spent on finding information. Modern search services for your applications, such as Azure Search, have improved dramatically by leveraging core AI techniques such as word embedding. More important, AI is also enabling a new type of search, usually characterized as *cognitive search*. Cognitive search leverages AI models to extract additional attributes from your assets, enabling new scenarios. For example, using an OCR model you can extract text from your documents in physical format and perform a search over them. Using an object detection model, you could enable a search on a repository of images in your organization. Using speech recognition, you could search for something mentioned in a video or a voice recording. Cognitive search can bring together all the structured and unstructured assets in your company and make them searchable and accessible to users. At Microsoft, we did an interesting experiment with cognitive search (*https://oreil.ly/AIO_2-11*) that you can access online: we applied these techniques to all the documents released on the assassination of John F. Kennedy, allowing users to not only search through the content, but also understand the entities, relationships, and even photographs included in the documents.

Creating New Applications with Conversational AI Interfaces

Of all the form factors enabled by AI, there's one that deserves special attention. Conversational interfaces, made possible by AI advancements in perception and cognition, are increasingly being seen in the application space as a strong option for human–computer interaction.

More than a use case of AI for the business, conversational interfaces provide a whole new canvas that can be applied to software portfolios in the enterprise. Just as the internet enabled a new form factor for applications—websites— AI is now enabling another form factor that will once again transform our engagement with employees and customers: *conversational agents*. And just as every organization created its own corporate website, organizations will now need to create their own corporate agents, both internal (employee-facing) and external (customer-facing).

Conversational agents are great for the transformation of technical departments, and for that reason they are picked by many companies as their first step in the AI organization journey. Conversational agents are relatively easy for existing application developers to embrace, and they can leverage a lot of the common backend services already in place in most organizations for web and mobile development.

However, conversational agents differ significantly from more traditional form factors in a few important ways:

- They require heavy use of AI technologies to provide a good user experience. Not only do they need to include strong natural language understanding capabilities, but they also need a range of cognition abilities to provide a natural interface.

- They are often expected to provide more than a transactional experience. A user's expectation for a website is to be able to perform transaction-based tasks like making a reservation or ordering a product. On the other hand, conversational agents are expected to support the same type of transaction-based requests ("Change my password"), as well as knowledge-based requests ("What computers do you recommend?") and even social chitchat ("Who created you?").

- They are exposed through a completely different set of channels. Conversational agents require a broad set of channels outside the well-established list of channels for your website or your mobile application. Customers and employees will expect your agents to be available in the channel of their choice—from existing conversational consumer platforms (such as Facebook Messenger or Skype) to enterprise collaboration solutions (such as Slack or Teams) to existing web or mobile applications—or even invokable from personal assistants like Alexa, Google Assistant, or Cortana.

APPROACHES TO YOUR CONVERSATIONAL AI STRATEGY

A great source of use cases for your conversational AI strategy is the application portfolio inventory mentioned earlier. Existing customer and employee interactions associated with your applications and website are great candidates for conversational agents. For the evaluation process, consider the following aspects:

- Start with narrow use cases (chatbots) and set the right expectations for the user. Conversational agents can be very disappointing if the scope is not clearly understood by the user. Developers can use available design guidance documents to follow this principle, like the one published by Microsoft Research (*https://oreil.ly/AIO_2-12*).

- Pick use cases that can specially benefit from a conversational AI. Decision flows (e.g., selecting a product), conditional data entry (e.g., describing an issue), and exploratory requests (e.g., learning options for an insurance contract) are good examples of use cases that can provide a better experience with a conversational interface.

- Prioritize use cases that are highly demanded but difficult to discover or time-consuming to perform. A good tactic to find these use cases is analyzing the traffic and search terms in your application or website, and the time spent finding the resource or performing the transaction itself.

This simple framework should give you a good list of low-hanging-fruit scenarios that you can address with narrow chatbots. Technical departments will learn in that process and you will get immediate return on your investment to keep the motivation high. In the case of Telefónica (*https://oreil.ly/AIO_2-13*), this low-hanging fruit was a chatbot integrated with the primary consumer mobile application in its O2 branch in the UK. The chatbot was able to attend to the most frequent requests from users in the app, including checking their bill, getting an update on their current data consumption, and getting information about their plan. For Unilever (*https://oreil.ly/AIO_2-14*), it was a chatbot that was able to deal with common requests that employees made to the HR department. In both cases, the systems were highly successful and provided a great experience for the technical teams.

However, you shouldn't stop there. Narrow use cases for conversational AI are just the beginning. As your technical organization gets more experience, you can address more complex scenarios.

OMNI-BOTS

A common approach for this gradual evolution is to bring together multiple narrow use cases into a broader agent—an "omni-bot." This concept allows easier management and maintenance, even by multiple teams. A dispatcher is able to redirect the requests appropriately to each individual chatbot based on the content, or it can send each request to all of them and pick the chatbot with the best match. This pattern is very common and supported by conversational AI platforms such as Azure Bot Service, and the resulting conversational agent can become a central hub for the entire organization.

At that point, organizations usually go one step further and provide some identity to the agent. Unilever, for example, is now creating a much broader internal agent centralizing multiple processes, called Una. Telefónica has created Aura, a personified agent centralizing all its services to customers.

The "hub" approach is not the only one used in complex agents. A promising approach to bot development is based on applying deep learning to the conversation itself to enable richer dialogues. Traditionally, bots process the user input turn by turn. Each command sent by the user is mapped to an intent using natural language understanding techniques. For example, "I want insurance for my car" could be mapped to the intent "Purchase insurance." The developer then manages the logic of what to do next, and the approach usually involves multi-turn dialogues that are designed manually. You can experience this by yourself if you follow the bot development exercise in Appendix A.

That technique is simple and works great for narrow bots or aggregations of narrow bots, but it doesn't scale for complex scenarios. A different approach to address these scenarios is to use a deep learning model to manage the conversation itself, and train it with past conversations as examples. This technique is available already in services such as Project Conversation Learner (*https://oreil.ly/*

AIO_2-15) and is an active area of development that will enable more complex agents (https://oreil.ly/AIO_2-16).

Think of customer support, for example. You can use logs of previous real support chats to train a generic model that can mimic those conversations, under the guidance of a business user. An option to escalate to a customer agent is provided if necessary, and the virtual agent can then support the customer support staff, increasing their productivity. This approach is already used by several companies, including HP (https://oreil.ly/AIO_2-17), which provides a chatbot on its support site, Macy's (https://oreil.ly/AIO_2-18), which handles user requests on its ecommerce site via a virtual customer support agent, and Microsoft, whose customer support chatbot covers hundreds of different use cases.

As more of these "omni-bots" are created, their level of sophistication will also increase. Users will expect these bots not only to attend to their commands, but also to be knowledgeable. Knowledge-based bots are able to answer questions in natural language, instead of just receiving commands. In the case of personal assistants these questions are usually related to personal life (movies, places, shopping, etc.), but in your corporate assistant, the questions will be related to your business. Several technologies are available today to help technical teams to create this kind of bot. At their core, these technologies are able to bring together unstructured or chaotic information from your internal systems and store it in a way that a bot can use to answer general questions in natural language. Azure QnA Maker (https://oreil.ly/AIO_2-19), for example, is able to take FAQ files already available in your organization and use them to answer similar questions in your bot.

When the level of complexity of your bot gets to this stage, you will notice an interesting effect. The requests received from your users will now not only be command-based or knowledge-based; they will be social. As the user gets more confident about the capabilities of the bot, human curiosity will start demanding more social conversations. Who hasn't asked Siri about a general topic?

When the agent gets to that level of interaction with your employees or your customers, you need to worry about a fascinating new topic: what personality do you want for your corporate presence? Do you want it to be casual? Funny? Serious? Companies at this level of maturity design bots with consistent and carefully planned personalities. Technology can help as well; Azure services like Project Personality Chat (https://oreil.ly/AIO_2-20) are providing promising results applying deep learning to chitchat conversations. Do you want your bot to behave like Harry Potter? You can train these services with Harry Potter's lines from the books.

OMNI-CHANNEL BOTS

As your organization creates broader use cases with conversational agents, your employees and customers will want to consume them on their channels of choice. Just like your corporate website can be accessed from any browser and device, conversational agents should be available on the platforms where your users are.

Omni-channel bots provide a consistent experience across all the channels, aligned with your corporate identity and services. Keep this in mind as your organization starts to create bots. It is easy to get started by creating just an Alexa skill or a web chatbot, but you will soon fall into the trap of creating a new bot for another channel, like Slack, Skype, or Google Assistant. Soon enough, you will be captive to that model and you will end up providing multiple inconsistent bots, each with an identity that aligns more with the provider of the channel than with your organization.

To avoid this, start with bots that are omni-channel from the get-go. Assume nothing about the channels. Today it may be web and Alexa. Tomorrow it could be WhatsApp and your custom device. Conversational AI platforms like Azure Bot Service or Google's Dialogflow are designed to be cross-channel and will make that process easier.

This approach will ensure that you have full control over your customer experience. Telefónica recently released Movistar Home (*https://oreil.ly/AIO_2-21*), an AI-powered device that replaces the landline devices in its customers' homes. Because Telefónica's digital assistant, Aura, is omni-channel, it could easily integrate with the device, owning the entire experience, services and data.

BMW also followed this approach for its in-car experience (*https://oreil.ly/AIO_2-22*). Instead of integrating a third-party personal assistant in its cars, the company created its own conversational agent with its own name, voice, and personality, providing a fully branded BMW experience. This end-to-end agent can give you directions, provide information about the car (like engine settings and tire pressure), and respond to voice commands (e.g., for climate control), even with no internet connectivity.

Such branded experiences can also integrate as needed with third-party personal assistants like Google Assistant and Cortana, but you keep control of that integration at all times; you control the full experience and what gets exposed.

From infusing existing applications with AI to creating entirely new experiences powered by AI like those we mentioned here, bringing AI to your technical departments is extremely powerful and will provide the necessary foundation for the next step in the journey for an AI organization: transforming your business units.

AI Hero: Athina

Athina's (*https://oreil.ly/AIO_3a-1*) fondest memories are of her time as a PhD student at the University of Sheffield, in the UK. She had just moved there from Greece, where she grew up, thanks to a scholarship. Athina still remembers how the university dean encouraged her to lecture as she worked on her PhD. Teaching is a powerful approach to learning. It makes you simplify concepts and try to make them interesting—and you get new perspectives from the students. Fifteen years later, now as the global head of AI at Accenture leading a team of 20,000 professionals, Athina still applies that same approach.

Athina joined Accenture to build its analytics capability, which then evolved to AI. As the only woman in the leadership team when she started, she describes that situation as a culture shock. Athina had felt extremely comfortable at university as a young female foreigner, where she taught postgraduate classes to students who in some cases were twice her age—but the open and collaborative nature of academia was very different from the private sector.

Athina was determined to shape her AI team at Accenture with the same culture she had experienced at university. First, she removed the hierarchical structure usually found in software integrators. Every analyst and every consultant had opportunities to present to leadership, because ideas and knowledge can come from anybody and anywhere. Removing hierarchical channels allows those ideas and that knowledge to flow directly to the leadership team, which is critical to driving innovation. The increased flexibility also encouraged more diverse hiring: Athina's data science team is now 38% women, with the goal of getting to 50% in the next two years.

Athina also applied to her team the principle her dean had encouraged in her: *teaching is learning.* She implemented a rotation plan in which team members can either take sabbaticals or work part time as university lecturers. Even inside the team, rotation is encouraged and employees can diversify their backgrounds and change disciplines.

This academic approach also applies to the way Athina's organization works with customers. Old-school consulting was primarily focused on outsourcing, but today's customers are hungry for knowledge. They want to be part of the journey, not just have a commercial transaction. In a sense, the contemporary relationship between consultants and customers is similar to the one between professors and students.

And that's exactly the culture Athina fostered in her organization, beginning with her team and then expanding it to the 475,000 employees at Accenture. AI, consulting, and strategy teams work together in pods, partnering with the customer in a business-first approach instead of the technology-first approach we discussed in the last chapter. The true potential of AI is to go beyond the technical teams and involve the business, transforming and reengineering every process in the organization.

To make that possible, Athina tells her customers that they need more than an AI team. They need translators in the business units, turning business needs into technology and AI insights into business decisions. With this approach, the consultant is a hub that guides that process, fostering thinking and discovery and providing the necessary knowledge and tools—just like a college professor.

The result of this approach has been an explosion of business use cases driven by AI that have the potential to redefine entire industries. Just in the last year (at the time of this writing) Athina's team has developed more than 10,000 proofs of concept across industries and functions, which turned into more than 1,000 industrialized use cases in production. Athina is also the executive sponsor of a program called Data Driven Consulting, an ambitious training program to make Accenture's consulting and strategy teams more data-driven in the discovery process with customers. They apply this framework in three primary domains with their customers:

Overall growth
> Rethinking the entire customer growth management process, from commercial activity to segmented marketing to basket analysis or customer support

Internal operations

Optimizing processes in areas such as HR (talent management, upskilling, recruiting, etc.) and finance (revenue forecast, investment management, growth areas identification, and so forth)

Industrial applications

Driving the next generation of manufacturing by leveraging the insights provided by the digitalization of industrial processes

Internally, Accenture is applying this framework to transform itself. For example, by partnering with the sales team, Athina's team created an AI solution that can predict a sales opportunity's likelihood of success with 97% accuracy. This allows sales representatives to combine their intuitive knowledge with the AI-powered insights to evaluate the 45,000 sales opportunities open at any one time, helping them make the decision of whether to pursue an opportunity or withdraw.

Externally, Athina's team has engaged with virtually every imaginable industry vertical. In the banking vertical, they applied this model to a global financial institution, identifying more than 400 use cases for AI. From those, they focused on the ones with the highest potential impact. For example, a crime-detection solution based on AI was able to provide $230 million in savings, with a reduction in false positives of 60%, and significantly improved compliance with global regulations. Other use cases targeted customer care. For example, the team developed a capability to interpret and understand customers' electronic documents and voice conversations to identify individuals in vulnerable situations like sickness or unemployment, who are then treated preferentially.

In oil and gas, the team worked with a top operator to create new ways of working across all parts of the business. More than 100 different types of AI models were created in a year, delivering significant value. One of them combined a production forecast for each of the operator's liquefied natural gas (LNG) plants with trading optimization, unlocking $100 million of value annually. AI-based well analytics identify patterns such as nonproductive time, drilling issues, and cost overruns, reducing the variance in estimation of well costs by 30%.

Working with a major telecommunications company in North America, Accenture developed an AI solution that guided customers to the right digital channel experience and acted as first-line support for the 500,000 customer care–related calls received every day. This decreased the number of calls agents had to answer by 30%, with a corresponding capital expenditure reduction of

$100 million per year. The improved customer experience also enabled a connection to product recommendations and sales, resulting in a sales conversion increase of 300%.

Low margins in consumer goods are also great candidates for AI-driven optimization. One of the largest beverage companies in the world was looking for a solution to optimize its pricing and trade agreements across all of its markets and retailers in Europe. In this case, the AI solution Accenture created provided insights and recommendations on strategies to follow that led an increase of 4.8% in net revenue growth from retailers and 10% in direct to consumer revenue.

All of these cases are examples of the impact that AI can bring to your business when applied to your core processes, which can happen only when technology and business units partner closely. It requires technical departments to transition from disconnected outsourcing centers to enablers that foster innovation in the business units. The staff take on the role of college professors looking to empower their students—the business—to flourish and transform.

In the next chapter, you will see in more detail how to make this connection happen, how to apply it to your own business processes, and how to identify the processes to target in your particular industry and organization.

## 3

The Business Transformation: Bringing AI to Every Business Process

Although an AI transformation can spring from a technology-first approach, the full impact of AI is best achieved if technology and business come together to rethink the primary functions in the organization. Every business process can be optimized or completely redefined with AI. The question is where to start.

Transforming Your Business Units

Just like the evaluation of potential scenarios in which you can bring AI to your applications, the first step in transforming your business is to inventory and categorize your processes. There are many frameworks in the industry for that, but I particularly like the one defined by management consultant and author Geoffrey Moore in his book *Zone to Win: Organizing to Compete in an Age of Disruption* (Diversion Books). Geoffrey states how every organization has to carefully balance four different zones:

Incubation
> Focused on evaluating multiple new opportunities enabled by new technology waves to identify future viable business options

Transformation
> Focused on scaling a particular disruptive opportunity identified in the incubation zone to a material revenue

Performance

Focused on maximizing the current primary revenue stream of the company

Productivity

Focused on delivering the programs and systems to support the performance zone

This model is very effective for understanding and balancing the different goals an organization has to pursue at any given time, and it applies perfectly to AI. As you identify potential use cases for AI you should always keep in mind the associated zone for each. A balanced strategy will address use cases that are representative of all four zones, so you can effectively transform your entire organization:

- The incubation zone will include moonshots enabled with AI. These moonshots are managed differently from other projects; they don't follow the same metrics (e.g., they are not pressured with short-term ROI goals) and are extremely agile and flexible.

- The transformation zone will focus on projects (ideally only one at a time) that are developed in the incubation zone, but are being scaled to the entire organization. These are moonshots that we bring to market. They need special attention and a strong push to escape the inertia of the existing business in the organization.

- The performance zone will focus on AI initiatives that can increase the revenue in the existing primary business. These initiatives can be managed at the existing rhythm of the business and follow the same ROI requirements and investment prioritization process.

- The productivity zone will contain use cases that can increase the effectiveness or decrease the costs of supporting processes. Just like in the performance zone, these use cases can be treated in the context of the existing processes for increasing the efficiencies in your organization.

As you prioritize the use cases in your organization, you will again have to consider the zones they belong to. Applying the same criteria for use cases in different zones is a common mistake that will result in an unbalanced approach for your strategy. If your main criterion is cost savings, you will end up with only use cases that are in the productivity zone, and you will miss potential areas where you can disrupt the business (or even worse, find yourself disrupted by competitors). The opposite is also true: focusing only on criteria that favor incubation projects will mean you miss opportunities to make your current business more competitive.

Identifying and Evaluating Use Cases

With that framework in mind, the next step is to identify as many use cases as possible, and evaluate them to prioritize the ones that are most relevant to your business. It is critical that this process be done in a partnership between the technical departments and the business units. Technical departments can bring AI to your applications on their own, but they cannot bring AI to business processes without the involvement of the business units. And that can happen only with the right internal structure and motivation.

A common approach is to create a multidisciplinary virtual team with representation from the technical departments and each of the business units. In some cases that isn't needed, especially if your organization is mature in its role as a software company, because there are already mechanisms in place to bring together technology and business—but no matter how you do it, the identification and evaluation of use cases for AI should be a joint exercise between the technical departments and business units. We'll discuss different organizational models to support that concept in more detail in Chapter 6.

Once the internal construct is in place, you can use the four zones (incubation, transformation, performance, and productivity) to identify the use cases in your organization. At Microsoft, we use a very simple framework to help customers in that process called *Agile Value Modeling*. In a highly iterative process between business and technology, projects are identified and distributed depending on their zone, with each represented with a bubble proportional to its potential value to the business.

The iterative nature of the process will help you to move through the quadrants to identify new projects to try. An incubation moonshot project may result in several smaller, tactical projects in the productivity area. A tactical project in the performance area can turn into a strategic transformational project. During the conversation, the business units and technical departments can help each other by sharing their different approaches:

From technology to business

Start with what AI can do. Basic training for the business users on the three primary types of AI capabilities (learning, perception, and cognition), as covered in the cheat sheet presented in Chapter 1, can be extremely helpful. They can then apply these concepts to their business model, with the technical members in the virtual team further defining the details iteratively.

From business to technology

Start with business scenarios, and jointly explore how they can be improved or redefined with AI. For example, business users can share the main challenges in the business, the long-term revenue plans, the primary cost drivers, and any other relevant considerations. A list of common use cases in organizations can be helpful for this approach; you can use one of the lists provided in this chapter as a starting point.

By now you should have a long list of potential business use cases for AI. It's now time to evaluate and prioritize them. Remember that it is critical to have representation across multiple zones, and the criteria for the prioritization should be modified depending on the zone. For incubation and transformation use cases, you should focus on criteria that favor the long-term opportunity:

Market differentiation

Will this use case create a strong, sustainable differentiation for the organization in the market?

Market opportunity

What total addressable market is associated with this use case?

Unique assets

What unique assets (data, processes, customer base, etc.) does the organization have to address this use case in a different way than its competitors?

Investment required

Can the organization sustain the long-term investment required to successfully develop the use case and move it to the transformation zone?

External disruptions

Is there an external disruption that the organization may miss out on if it doesn't target this use case? What is the potential negative impact of that?

Network effect
> Can this use case ignite a virtuous cycle with exponential growth?

For performance and productivity use cases, you should focus on criteria that favor short-term impact and viability:

Cost
> What is the estimated cost of the implementation, including internal and external resources?

Return on investment
> How profitable can we estimate the use case to be, in terms of incremental sales, reduced costs, productivity gains, or improved quality?

Payback period
> What's the estimated time it will take for the investment to pay for itself?

Nonmaterial impact
> What other metrics might be affected by the use case (customer satisfaction, loyalty, brand perception, increased barriers for competitors, etc.)?

Risk
> How likely is the implementation of the use case to be successful? What dependencies and uncertainties are involved?

Readiness
> Is the organization in a good position to implement this use case? Does it have the necessary resources (data, infrastructure, human resources, organizational resources) for it?

These criteria should provide a good framework for the combined technical and business team to evaluate potential use cases and discuss them with the company's management. However, at the end of the day, the final prioritization should be based on the organization's expertise. Never underestimate the power of intuition or of the passion of the team behind the idea. Making the person or team that proposes an idea the "CEO" of that idea is a powerful concept that can make a big difference to its success.

The criteria used should also drive the definition of success. Learning is as important as implementing the use cases themselves, and we won't learn if we don't measure the success of each initiative we target. Consider the following areas when establishing the metrics for your AI use cases:

Metrics associated with the business impact

These are closely aligned to your selection criteria and they are different for projects in each of the four zones. Some examples of business impact metrics are adoption, revenue, cost savings, and productivity increase.

Quality metrics

You'll want to measure the level of quality of the final product, as well as its evolution. Metrics in this group can include the accuracy of the system, user satisfaction, deployment ratios, and volume of support incidents.

Metrics related to the implementation

To improve future execution and readiness, you should also measure the implementation itself: for example, schedule performance, budget performance, employee satisfaction, and completeness of requirements.

These metrics should be carried throughout the entire lifecycle of the project and owned by the entire multidisciplinary team associated with it. As you will learn in Chapter 5, a team that is aligned with the business outcomes of a project is the essence of a successful AI implementation.

Typical AI Use Cases

The following sections present a selection of popular use cases for you to use as inspiration. They are separated into two categories of business processes:

- *Horizontal processes*, which are similar across any industry. These are well-known functions like marketing, sales, or HR. The use cases behind these functions are usually in the performance and productivity areas. They won't disrupt your business, but they can provide ideas for low-risk, short-term projects. In many cases, you can even leverage an out-the-box solution from a third-party provider, or reusable artifacts like accelerators or AI models.

- *Vertical processes*, which are unique to your industry vertical (such as manufacturing, health care, or retail). These processes are usually highly unique in every organization, and they rely on years of expertise, IP, and proprietary datasets. They have a strong potential to disrupt your business and increase your differentiation, but they are higher-risk, longer-term projects involving custom AI development.

We will start by covering use cases for the primary horizontal business functions. Then we'll look at vertical use cases, and I'll provide examples from different industries. (Feel free to jump directly to the section that covers your industry; I won't be offended!)

Each use case is mapped to the primary AI capability that you will use to implement it. Looking at use cases like "predictive maintenance" or "sales forecasting" can be useful to provide inspiration for a "business to technology" approach, whereas focusing on AI capabilities like "vision" or "classification" can help you find new ideas for the "technology to business" approach. Either way, you can use these lists as inspiration while strengthening the deep partnership between business and technology required to identify the best use cases for your own company.

Horizontal Processes

As mentioned previously, horizontal processes are well-known business functions that span industries, such as marketing, IT, and customer service. Microsoft itself is going through a transformation of those functions, so I'll share examples of our own journey for each of them.

MARKETING

Marketing is probably the function in any company that has experienced the biggest digital transformation in recent years. Digital marketing now accounts for a significant part of most companies' marketing resources, and even traditional advertisement is heavily driven by data nowadays. With that strong digital foundation, it's not a surprise that marketing is a function with so much potential for AI.

AI is great at providing insights into the immense amount of data generated by marketing activities. Table 3-1 lists some of the most common use cases for this scenario, along with the primary AI capability enabling each of them.

Table 3-1. Marketing insights use cases

Use case	AI capability
Brand insights: Understand in real time how customers are talking about your brand, identifying sentiment and extracting key topics and drivers.	A字 Natural Language
Customer insights: Identify customer segments, patterns, and trends in customer interests by analyzing sources such as search engines, social media, etc.	Pattern Recognition
PR analytics: Understand the impact of your own PR activities and those of your competitors, identifying themes and sentiment.	A字 Natural Language
Feedback insights: Centralize the feedback channels in the company (email, social media, websites, etc.) and identify hot topics and dissatisfaction drivers.	A字 Natural Language

In other cases, AI not only can inform us so that we can make better decisions, but directly act on our behalf to optimize our marketing activities. Table 3-2 gives some examples.

Table 3-2. Marketing optimization use cases

Use case	AI capability
Campaign optimization: Use AI to optimize the customers targeted or the content used, maximizing the conversion rates.	Optimization
Retargeting: Identify the best content and next actions to reach customers who have engaged previously with another marketing activity.	Recommendation
Personalization: Customize the marketing content (emails, web experience, communications) based on customer data to retain or upgrade customers.	Optimization

Use case	AI capability
Social automation: Provide a first level of automation for common interactions in social media or feedback channels.	A字 Natural Language

Beyond insights and actions, AI can also have a strong impact in the transition from marketing to sales. A few examples of this are given in Table 3-3.

Table 3-3. Sales conversion use cases

Use case	AI capability
Lead scoring: Identify the marketing opportunities with higher sales probabilities to optimize the leads that are passed to sales and decide on the channel for each.	Classification
Account-based marketing: Identify marketing surges in an account, and proactively provide opportunity information to the corresponding sellers.	Classification

Microsoft uses a lot of these scenarios internally with positive results. Our Global Demand Center, which centralizes our customer acquisition and engagement marketing engine globally, has been using AI to optimize the leads passed to sales. Fake contacts (*https://oreil.ly/AIO_3-1*) are removed with AI, and opportunities are scored and ranked with thousands of variables in real time. Following qualification, marketing hands off the leads to the appropriate sales channels. Using this approach, nonworkable leads were reduced by two-thirds and conversion rates increased 108% year over year (*https://oreil.ly/AIO_3-2*).

SALES

AI not only can improve the number and quality of the leads passed to sales, it can also help during the sales process itself. This can be done by directly assisting the sellers in tasks such as those listed in Table 3-4.

Table 3-4. Seller assistance use cases

Use case	AI capability
Pipeline prioritization: Identify customers in the pipeline at risk of churn or likely to move the opportunity forward with an action.	Classification
Cold call lists: Generate customer lists for cold calls, identifying fit with product offerings, upselling opportunities, or renewal opportunities.	Classification
Next best action: Recommend the best potential next action by the seller for a specific account, given the past actions and the pipeline state.	Recommendation
Meeting assistance: Provide guidance to the seller prior to a meeting or presentation to a customer, with context, opportunities, and recommended approaches.	Recommendation

AI can also be effective for broader scenarios that may be relevant to sales management (see Table 3-5).

Table 3-5. Sales management use cases

Use case	AI capability
Sales forecasting and quota setting: Predict the team's sales forecast based on internal and external conditions for reporting purposes or quota setting.	Regression
Best practice identification: Analyze behaviors and practices correlated to top sales, to implement as best practices in the team.	Pattern Recognition

Microsoft's extensive number of cloud services and diverse portfolio for enterprises require a thorough understanding of the customer's needs at all times so that the conversation is relevant for the customer and aligned with their interests. An AI application called Daily Recommender (*https://oreil.ly/AIO_3-3*) helps every seller at Microsoft to attain their quota by predicting the likelihood of a customer to buy products, consume services, or churn. Sellers get recommendations on each customer, including content to share, email templates, and call scripts. This approach increased the recommendation success rate fourfold, resulting in a 40% recommendation-to-opportunity rate.

FINANCE

Finance is undergoing a transformation, from a pure operational function to a proactive, forward-looking partner for the rest of the business. AI can play a role in that transformation, elevating finance within the organization in a number of ways (see Table 3-6).

Table 3-6. Finance use cases

Use case	AI capability
Demand planning: Anticipate the demand for products or services to manage inventory, investments, or geographical distribution.	Regression
Revenue forecasting: Complement traditional approaches to forecasting with AI-based methods based on historical sales data, information about deals in progress, and external conditions.	Regression
Compliance: Optimize auditing practices to automatically identify high-risk transactions before they are closed and detect process anomalies.	Classification
Expense reporting: Increase employee productivity for common financial processes such as expense reporting, and help automate the processing and auditing.	Classification
Contract management: Understand and mine contracts in the organization, identifying contract obligations and auditing contract terms.	Natural Language

Finance was actually one of the first organizations in Microsoft to apply AI internally. The company's revenue has been forecast with AI (*https://oreil.ly/ AIO_3-4*) for several years now, with quite accurate results. Predictions are centralized and exposed with custom views for each role. For instance, sellers can gain insights on actuals versus forecasts by segments, subsegments, pricing levels, and products. After implementing AI, the variance between our overall revenue forecasts and actuals reduced from 3% to 1.5%, and this variance was reduced even more in businesses with a lot of transactions, such as those in the small or medium business space. After this success, Microsoft Finance began using AI extensively in other processes, such as compliance analytics, anomaly detection, and text analytics on global economy documents like company earnings and government reports.

HUMAN RESOURCES

HR is another example of a function within many companies that's transforming from the earlier model of a reactive, process-oriented cost center to a more proactive and strategic function at the service of the business and the employees. AI can make core processes in HR more productive, so HR agents can focus on high-value activities. Table 3-7 gives some examples of core processes that can be augmented with AI.

Table 3-7. HR use cases

Use case	AI capability
Hiring: Support the identification of appropriate candidates or discover potential candidates either internally or externally.	Classification
Subject matter expert (SME) identification: Support or automate the skill profiling in an organization to better match employees with projects, enable employees to connect with SMEs, or identify the right contacts for customers, projects, or products.	Classification
Retention risk assessment: Predict retention risks in employees to enable early engagement and improve job satisfaction.	Classification
HR analytics: Understand the organization's health in real time by monitoring employee feedback, coming either from regular pulses across the organization or from proactive feedback.	Natural Language
Employee support: Increase HR agent productivity by automating common HR requests and tasks with conversational assistants.	Natural Language
Smart buildings: Improve office building management, access control, and efficiency by combining sensors and AI.	Optimization

At Microsoft, we aim to transform HR by providing employees with what they need in real time. For instance, we've created an HR bot that can automate common tasks requested by employees, like the creation of more than 5,000 travel letters every month. Employees' offices at the Microsoft campus use AI to optimize energy consumption, do preventative maintenance, and even predict employees' complaints on temperature conditions and act before they're made.

IT AND SOFTWARE DEVELOPMENT

Technical departments play an important role in the overall AI transformation in the company, but they can also leverage AI for their existing functions. Internal IT operations can benefit from AI in multiple processes, as illustrated in Table 3-8.

Table 3-8. IT use cases

Use case	AI capability
Security protection: Analyze activity and behavioral data inside the organization to identify bad practices and security attacks.	Classification
Helpdesk bots: Provide conversational agents for employees to get automated support for the common cases.	A字 Natural Language
Datacenter management: Optimize the utilization, energy efficiency, reliability, and performance of on-premises datacenters.	Optimization

Software development can also benefit from AI applied to the tools and services used by developers, as shown in Table 3-9.

Table 3-9. Software development use cases

Use case	AI capability
Developer assistance: Provide advanced capabilities based on AI in development tools to improve productivity, such as smart autocompletion or code generation.	Recommendation
Bug detection and fixing: Automatically detect bugs in the source code for applications, and either provide recommendations or directly fix the issues.	Natural Language
DevOps automation: Apply AI in the DevOps cycle to detect issues in production and identify the code responsible for them, decreasing the mean time to repair.	Classification
Security analysis: Identify security vulnerabilities in the code and propose remedies.	Classification

Being a technology company, Microsoft has implemented many of these use cases for its own software development, and there are many others that it provides to its customers. Azure itself uses AI heavily to manage aspects such as hardware health prediction, resource optimization, performance, and utilization. AI is also infused into the DevOps processes at Microsoft, helping developers analyze their telemetry data and even suggesting appropriate fixes for issues.

In the realm of security, Microsoft uses AI to detect phishing attempts, protect against malware, and identify security threats, analyzing more than 6.5 trillion global signals each day. Microsoft Security Risk Detection (*https://oreil.ly/ AIO_3-5*) uses AI to discover security bugs in software; it was responsible for finding one-third of the "million dollar" security bugs in Windows 7.

For software development, Microsoft is already making available many of the internal tools for any developer to use. The latest version of Visual Studio includes many features powered by AI for developer productivity. The AI can be trained on the vast repository of open source public code on GitHub or your own company's code, and it provides features like smart code completion and assisted code reviews.

CUSTOMER SERVICE

Customer service is probably one of the first functions explored by most organizations looking to bring AI into the business. They are looking for approaches that can create a better customer experience, identify customer dissatisfaction issues, and help customer agents be more productive. Table 3-10 lists some of the use cases typically addressed for customer service.

Table 3-10. Customer service use cases

Use case	AI capability
Intelligent routing: Automatically identify the right agent or department for a customer service interaction, given the intent provided by the customer and their past history.	Classification
Virtual agents: Resolve customer support issues with automated virtual agents that can interact naturally with conversational AI, or escalate to a customer agent if needed.	Natural Language
Issue identification: Quickly identify and respond to emerging trends in customer support and proactively address them.	Natural Language
Customer agent assistance: Augment customer agents by providing automatic suggestions during the customer interaction.	Natural Language
Churn prediction: Identify customers likely to churn in real time during support interactions.	Classification
Call analysis: Analyze customer interaction logs and surveys to identify best practices for customer satisfaction and increase efficiencies.	Natural Language

At Microsoft, we have implemented several AI-based solutions (*https://oreil.ly/AIO_3-6*) across our support organization. One of them is able to flag a case as high risk based on multiple indicators from past interactions. This enables the agent to prepare for a call even more thoroughly when needed, or pass the case to another agent with deeper expertise on the topic. Customer interaction and feedback analysis is used to coach the support team and identify unresolved cases. Recovery managers contact those customers to ensure a resolution, driving a 180% average increase in sentiment score compared with the initial interactions.

Finally, we also provide a virtual agent that fields customer queries in our support center. The AI chat experience covers a broad range of products including Windows, Office, and Xbox. It can converse in complex multiturn dialogues that require comprehension and reasoning. It then offers instant answers and recommends actions to solve the issue, or it escalates it to a customer agent (who will be assisted as well by the virtual agent). Since its launch, the virtual agent has handled more than 100,000 support cases per day, with an increase in customer satisfaction of 31% and a 3x reduction of agent-to-agent transfers because of the intelligent routing.

Vertical Processes

We have explored many horizontal processes, with examples of how we have addressed some of them in our AI transformation at Microsoft. Because these processes are shared across industries, they are likely to also be candidates for your organization. But what about your unique processes? Those depend on your industry and your company's unique expertise, and they have the potential to increase your differentiation and even disrupt your market. In this section, you will find real examples of customers redefining these vertical processes. Use these examples as inspiration, but ultimately finding these types of use cases for your organization requires deep exploration in partnership between technical departments and business units.

MANUFACTURING

Manufacturing is a great example of an industry that has been radically transformed by technology over the past century. The three industrial revolutions—steam, electric power, and electronics—were all born in manufacturing, so it's no surprise that it's one of the industries with the fastest adoption of the fourth industrial revolution: AI.

The ongoing digitization of manufacturing through the Internet of Things (IoT) provides real-time data that can be combined with AI to create the concept of a smart factory. However, the impact of AI can go beyond the factory and include other areas such as product design or supply chain management (see Table 3-11).

Table 3-11. Manufacturing use cases

Use case	AI capability
Predictive maintenance: Analyze the data generated by sensors in the equipment to predict when maintenance should be performed, instead of sticking to ineffective time-based maintenance schedules.	Regression
Quality assurance: Use perception techniques such as vision to identify defective products in the manufacturing line.	Vision
Industrial safety: Identify risks or safety violations in the factory to prevent worker accidents, typically using computer vision.	Vision
Autonomous systems: Optimize systems with automatic self-control, such as power generators or HVAC systems, or enable more complex and autonomous industrial robots and vehicles.	Planning
Supply chain management: Increase efficiencies in the supply chain and mitigate disruptions with risk prediction.	Optimization
Demand forecasting: Anticipate demand increases or decreases based on external factors to optimize production.	Regression
Generative product design: Apply AI in the product design stage to generate multiple options meeting the goals and identify the most effective and optimized design.	Optimization
Digital twins: Create a virtual model of a product, process, or even an entire factory to monitor and analyze the system. Combined with simulations, digital twins can also help you understand the impact of potential conditions or assess future opportunities.	Regression

Jabil is a global manufacturing company spanning numerous industries such as consumer products, networking, and aerospace. Jabil was able to optimize its factory operations to be more competitive by connecting its equipment, sensors, and people. The company also uses AI perception capabilities to improve its processes: for example, automated optical inspection in the production line scans for any sign of defects, ensuring all potential anomalies are detected early.

In addition, Jabil analyzes millions of data points from machines running dozens of steps to predict failures earlier in the process. Using AI, the company was able to achieve 80% accuracy (*https://oreil.ly/AIO_3-7*) in the prediction of machine slowdowns or failures. Its AI solution is not only able to predict a condition, but also to explain why it was predicted, allowing Jabil to optimize its operations to avoid these conditions in the future.

FINANCIAL SERVICES

Financial technology, or fintech, is already disrupting traditional banking. The internet and mobile devices transformed every single frontend and back office process, from deposits to small payments, loans to insurance, trading to portfolio management.

New players are entering the market, benefiting from this transformation and the low barrier of entry provided by technologies such as the cloud and blockchain. These new players are putting enormous pressure on the incumbent players, redefining the industry with new approaches such as peer-to-peer lending, crowdfunding, and mobile payments. Traditional banking now has to balance a heavily regulated and supervised industry with the agility and nimbleness of those startups disrupting the market.

AI can leverage the deep digital transformation already in place in the industry to create a new layer of differentiation from competitors and new players. A common starting point for AI in financial services is the customer-focused processes that are already being transformed. Table 3-12 gives some examples.

Table 3-12. Customer process use cases

Use case	AI capability
"Just in time" lending: Apply AI techniques to accelerate the risk assessment process for credit applications.	Classification
Default prediction: Improve accuracy of risk assessment, which can be used to increase revenue by issuing loans that previously would have been denied or by anticipating and avoiding defaults.	Classification

Use case	AI capability
Dynamic pricing: Apply machine learning to broader data assets to provide more accurate pricing and optimize underwriting. For example, drivers can voluntarily provide sensor data in their vehicles to reward their driving practices with AI.	Optimization
Claim processing: Use techniques like natural language processing or computer vision to expedite and optimize claim processing.	Natural Language
Personalized banking: Provide customized services such as portfolio management, savings advice based on customer habits, or tailored reward incentives using AI-powered recommendation techniques, often also accessed through conversational AI.	Recommendation

However, the impact of AI in financial services is deeper than the customer-focused scenarios, and has the potential of redefining core back office processes. Some examples are given in Table 3-13.

Table 3-13. Core process use cases

Use case	AI capability
Fraud detection: Use AI to spot unusual patterns by analyzing multiple data points to identify fraudulent transactions that rule-based analysis may miss.	Classification
Compliance assurance: Analyze structured transactions in conjunction with unstructured data such as documents, emails, or voice orders to identify internal practices compromising compliance.	Classification
Trading and investment management: Optimize trade execution strategies and mergers and acquisitions analysis, augmenting agents and analysts with intelligent insights across multiple data sources.	Optimization
Trend identification and simulation: Mine vast amounts of unstructured data from economic reports, company earnings, news, social media, and other sources to identify trends that can impact the investment portfolio, or simulate conditions to assess a potential impact on it.	Natural Language

QuarterSpot (*https://oreil.ly/AIO_3-8*) is an online lending platform for small businesses that uses advanced models that incorporate real-time data from various sources—including business bank accounts—to assess applicant risk. Based on the results, QuarterSpot decides on whether to approve the loan and the appropriate interest rate for the risk. QuarterSpot then posts the loan in its marketplace, where investors can purchase portions of that loan in increments of $25.

For a model like this to work, QuarterSpot needed to drastically reduce the time taken to accurately predict the risk and approve a loan. To achieve both goals, the company applied AI models that were continuously improved in an agile MLOps cycle (covered in detail in Chapter 6). In just two years QuarterSpot was able to lower default rates by more than 50%, while increasing borrower approval rates by more than 15% and decreasing lending costs by 83% compared with traditional methods. Today, QuarterSpot also provides its AI models to more traditional lenders through a lending platform, creating an entire new business model for the organization.

RETAIL

If there's a single sector that knows what technology disruption means, it's retail. Ecommerce revolutionized the sector's core services, introduced new players in the market, and forever changed customer expectations. Today, retailers have to compete with born-in-the-cloud players like Amazon, which can utilize its digital footprint to mine data on purchases and customer preferences to offer an extremely personalized and effective experience. Shoppers are now demanding similar (if not better) experiences from traditional retailers, which must create their own intelligent experiences with the added complexity of a hybrid physical/ online store presence.

It is, however, within that diversity of channels that retailers are finding an interesting area to provide a differentiated value. AI can be applied to the online presence, but it can also be used to redefine the physical presence and extend it to the online sphere, offering a unique value proposition for customers through a multichannel, seamless experience.

For the online presence, there are multiple well-known AI scenarios already familiar to users. Table 3-14 gives some examples.

Table 3-14. Online retail use cases

Use case	AI capability
Product recommendation: Automatically provide relevant product recommendations for the user depending on their past behavior, including previous purchases, viewing history, explicit ratings, or any other customer signal.	Recommendation
Personalization: Customize the online experience and/or outbound marketing content (e.g., emails, discounts, rewards) based on the customer's behaviors and preferences.	Recommendation
AI-assisted product discovery: Assist shoppers with intelligent tools such as visual search, virtual dressing rooms, or conversational AI to help them narrow down their selection and recommend products based on their needs, preferences, and fit.	Vision

But by expanding these scenarios to physical stores, retailers can differentiate themselves from online-only competitors. Table 3-15 contains some examples.

Table 3-15. Physical store use cases

Use case	AI capability
Personalized storefronts: Adapt physical elements such as product displays or customer service to provide a personalized experience for each visitor in the physical store, connected to their online identity.	Recommendation
Automatic or assisted checkout: Use AI techniques such as computer vision or a multisensor environment to optimize the checkout process, or remove it entirely.	Vision
Shopping list assistance: Analyze past purchases to understand behavior, automatically offering shopping lists that can then be customized by the user.	Recommendation
Store monitoring and analysis: Employ computer vision to identify user behavior, optimize product placement, and support store employees with real-time notifications on restocking, spill accidents, or aisle congestion.	Vision

Retailers can also leverage AI to optimize their operations across both their online and physical channels. Table 3-16 presents some examples.

Table 3-16. Retail operations use cases

Use case	AI capability
Operational optimization: Use AI to optimize logistical aspects such as staffing, supply chains, or inventory.	Optimization
Demand forecasting: Analyze external data such as consumer interest, share of voice, and competitor insights to improve demand prediction, redistribution, and inventory management.	Regression
Dynamic pricing: Establish product pricing and personalized discounts in real time based on factors such as competitor pricing, demand estimation, user shopping habits, and external factors.	Optimization
Responsive design: Interpret customer feedback, sentiment, and purchasing data to support the design of future products and services.	Natural Language

Kroger is America's largest grocery retailer. It's a great example of a traditional retailer reimagining the customer experience across its physical and online channels, connecting them in a seamless experience powered by AI through the EDGE Shelf technology (*https://oreil.ly/AIO_3-9*), a shelving system that uses digital displays instead of traditional paper tags. Kroger centralizes the data captured in its physical stores and through its web and mobile applications to optimize the customer experience in the stores, including the ability to optimize pricing in near real time.

Kroger can also provide unique experiences to its customers with this technology. The electronic shelves can use customer preference data, personalized promotions, and shopping lists to provide a unique guided shopping experience for customers.

Using video analytics, Kroger is also able to assist its store employees with restocking, notify them of incidents like spills, and even help them optimize product placement or provide custom advertisements based on customer demographics. For example, a family shopping together could receive recommendations for certain promotions on the digital shelves as they walk down an aisle.

PUBLIC SECTOR

When thinking about the public sector, one of the first areas that comes to mind is efficiency. The amount of procedures that the public administration has to manage for citizens and businesses is a burden that often limits the high-value services that could be provided. Repetitive procedures are a paradise for AI and present a great opportunity to obtain short-term benefits, as the examples in Table 3-17 demonstrate.

Table 3-17. Public sector productivity use cases

Use case	AI capability
Data entry automation: Optimize data entry processes across multiple applications and systems with techniques such as robotic process automation that can learn from the manual data entry to generalize the process and automate it.	Planning
Information search: Apply AI to the vast amount of unstructured data (such as documents and forms) in public administrations such as justice departments, local governments, and centralized institutions to extract knowledge or enable easy search and navigation, both internally and for citizens.	Natural Language
Tax management: Optimize the processes to simplify tax submissions and identify fraud and suspicious activities.	Classification
Process optimization: Automatically route and monitor service requests from citizens, optimizing time and resources.	Optimization

Beyond the foundational administrative services, public institutions also manage massive quantities of assets. AI can help optimize this. Table 3-18 lists some examples.

Table 3-18. Public sector optimization use cases

Use case	AI capability
Fleet management: Use AI techniques to forecast demand for public transportation to better distribute and manage fleets in real time.	Optimization

Use case	AI capability
Public safety: Develop criminal activity forecasting for better public-safety asset distribution.	Regression
Education: Predict dropouts or identify specific needs to develop customized curricula or provide additional support.	Classification
Smart cities: Use sensors and IoT devices to monitor city assets such as power, transportation, or water supply, as well as environmental data such as noise levels, air quality, or weather. When those resources are digitally monitored, AI can be used to optimize resources, identify patterns, or predict events.	Optimization
City digital twins: Smart cities are usually combined with the concept of a digital twin. A digital twin is a virtual representation of a physical entity, in this case a city. IoT devices can capture information in real time from the physical city that can be used to replicate it in a virtual environment. AI can use this virtual representation to simulate new conditions and analyze the impact, helping local authorities prepare for special events or optimize future public investments.	Optimization

Probably the most visible scenario in which AI is applied in the public sector is to transform the relationship of a government with its citizens. Just as it can redefine the interactions between companies and customers, AI can also bring government closer to citizens in multiple ways, such as those listed in Table 3-19.

Table 3-19. Citizen interaction use cases

Use case	AI capability
Conversational assistants for citizens: Use conversational interfaces to guide citizens through service requests, provide general information, or assist on city services such as transportation.	Natural Language
Social listening: Understand citizen's opinions, sentiment, and complaints using natural language understanding techniques on social media and any other feedback channel.	Natural Language
Tourism promotion: Enhance the experience for tourists through multilanguage assistance, augmented experiences for points of interest, or informational bots.	Natural Language

The City of Los Angeles provides a conversational assistant (*https://oreil.ly/ AIO_3-10*) called Chip (City Hall Internet Personality) that can gather and present a collection of information about any given topic or area, outline city resources and opportunities that are available to residents, and assist with filling out forms.

One of the states in Southern India, Andhra Pradesh, minimizes school dropout rates in more than 10,000 schools by using AI to predict dropouts (*https://oreil.ly/AIO_3-11*), enabling early intervention by personnel.

Imec, a leading R&D and innovation hub in nanoelectronics and digital technologies, has partnered with Antwerp to launch a digital twin (*https://oreil.ly/ AIO_3-12*) of the Belgian city. The digital 3D replica is created with real-time sensor information providing feedback on air quality, traffic, and noise pollution. AI provides a predictive view of the situation in the city where the impact of planned measures can be simulated and tested, to understand, for example, how an action by the city planners might impact traffic, noise levels, or air quality.

HEALTH CARE

Despite the infinite possibilities that AI brings to every industry vertical, health care is without a doubt the one for which it has the biggest potential to have a positive impact on society. The amount of data available in the health care sector, most of it highly unstructured, can now be leveraged at scale to redefine medicine. Table 3-20 provides some examples.

Table 3-20. Advanced health care use cases

Use case	AI capability
Image diagnosis: Augment and scale specializations such as radiology, oncology, or ophthalmology with AI applied to medical image analysis, helping with diagnosis, improving treatment and surgery planning, and bringing health care to populations without access to specialists.	Vision
Medical record mining: Analyze the vast amount of unstructured data in medical records, including test results, medical images, and doctor's notes, to identify patterns that can help diagnose a disease and recommend the next best actions.	Natural Language
Precision medicine: Combine AI with genomics to treat patients individually with customized treatments that are optimized for their genetic content, predicting which drug will produce the best effect for a patient.	Recommendation

Use case	AI capability
Predictive care: Detect the likelihood of a disease based on the patient's genome, symptoms, blood samples, or any other personal information. Then proactively intervene with preventive medicine, treatments, or lifestyle changes.	Classification
Drug development: Assist scientists in the drug discovery process, by either facilitating access to the vast amount of information needed for drug creation or optimizing the process of clinical trials by prioritizing potential molecular structures to focus on.	Classification

These use cases have huge potential to redefine medicine as we know it, but AI can also improve the most mundane processes and operations, enabling short-term results for a better patient and professional experience (see Table 3-21).

Table 3-21. Health care professionals use cases

Use case	AI capability
Personal health assistants: Use conversational AI technologies to assist patients with monitoring and treatment, provide first-level advice based on symptoms and medical history, or coach patients with chronic diseases or risk conditions on lifestyle habits.	Natural Language
Dictation assistance: Assist health professionals with capturing documentation, using speech-to-text techniques to automatically enter the information in the electronic health record (EHR) systems. Use natural language processing to extract knowledge, such as symptoms, and assist health professionals with follow-up explorations and diagnosis candidates.	Natural Language
Remote monitoring: Combine AI with IoT devices to perform remote monitoring of recovering patients or at-risk populations such as the elderly, people with disabilities, or chronic patients.	Classification
Physical facility optimization: Optimize constrained resources in hospitals and other facilities by estimating progression of inpatients through the system, optimally redistributing staff, and predicting readmissions or bounce-backs in advance to minimize them.	Optimization

BlueMetal, an Insight company specializing in health care solutions, worked with Steward Healthcare (*https://oreil.ly/AIO_3-13*) to predict the length of patients' hospital stays to help doctors and nurses with schedule planning. The same system is able to use external factors such as seasonality and flu activity and other data sources such as the CDC social media to predict with 98% accuracy what their volumes will look like one and two weeks out, enabling the planning and optimization of hospital resources.

BlueMetal also partnered with Vivli (*https://oreil.ly/AIO_3-14*), a nonprofit organization focused on sharing individual participant data from clinical trials, to work on a solution involving AI techniques to allow all this global data to be easily searched and analyzed, accelerating scientific discovery for health care.

Adaptive Biotechnologies (*https://oreil.ly/AIO_3-15*) is combining AI with the recent breakthroughs in biotechnology to map and decode the human immune system. With this technique, the company is aiming to create a universal blood test that reads a person's immune system to detect a wide variety of diseases in the earliest stages, including infections, cancers, and autoimmune disorders.

Aurora Health Care is a nonprofit health care system with 15 hospitals and more than 150 clinics. With its conversational AI experience (*https://oreil.ly/AIO_3-16*) users can answer a set of questions about themselves and the symptoms they are experiencing; the AI agent adapts to the answers with follow-up questions, provides possible causes, and suggests a next action, including whether the patient should go to urgent care or see their primary doctor. The virtual concierge can even schedule the appointment directly from within the conversational experience.

The examples discussed here across horizontal and vertical processes highlight the breadth of use cases that business units can target in any organization. But what if we enable not only business units but *every employee* to create and target their own scenarios? We'll explore that concept in the next chapter—but first, let's take a look at Tanya's story, which embodies this idea.

AI Hero: Tanya

"It's easier to ask forgiveness than it is to get permission." We've probably all heard that quote, but only a few know its origin. Tanya (*https://oreil.ly/AIO_4a-1*) is one of them, and I learned it from her. The quote belongs to Grace Hopper (*https://oreil.ly/AIO_4a-2*), a US Naval officer who is considered a pioneer of computer programming. She created the first compiler for a programming language, which evolved into the incredibly popular COBOL, which is still behind many of the largest applications in the world (like core banking systems).

Hopper's idea was simple: instead of humans needing to learn the language of computers to program them, why don't computers learn ours? Hopper's compiler was designed to translate English-based language with instructions like IF, SET, STOP, or JUMP to a set of machine instructions that a computer would understand.

If there was one thing that Rear Admiral Hopper hated the most, it was hearing a sentence popular in every organization on the planet: "We've always done it this way." When sharing her idea with others, she heard that expressed in many forms. "Computers could only do arithmetic, they could not do programs," she was told.

There are some people in this world who get more motivated to do something when they are told their idea can't be implemented. These people see something that is broken, and they fix it—no permission required. Grace Hopper was one of them. Tanya, a professor at the University of Illinois and the cofounder of the AI nonprofit Wild Me, is definitely another.

In Tanya's case, that approach to life started early. She grew up in the Soviet Union during the perestroika political movement. Led by Mikhail Gorbachev, the perestroika involved a transformation in the economic system as well as an increase in the openness and transparency of government (or "glasnost"). A side effect of this movement was the exacerbation of existing political, territorial, and social tensions within the Soviet Union. That included, unfortunately, a rise in anti-Semitism and nationalism.

Being a Jewish woman, Tanya had people question her ambitions from a very young age. Administrators at a high school for gifted kids in Leningrad (now St. Petersburg) tried to block her admission (and later, after she had been admitted, to expel her on 19 occasions), just because she was a Jew.

The language and literature teacher at that same high school was also the spokesperson for the anti-Semitic nationalist organization Pamyat ("memory"). Tanya had to read leaflets her teacher had written that contained explicit anti-Semitic statements, and listen to xenophobic essays from other students in that teacher's class. In a country where your ethnic group was in the third column on the class roster, right after your first and last names, it was only a matter of time before something horrible happened.

And it did. One day, Tanya was beaten badly by a group of drunk students. She came back to school after recovering, and describing what happened next still causes her voice to break 30 years later. All the students in her class went on strike to support her—all 28 of them. This was the first student strike known in the perestroika, and it immediately captured the attention of the national media. Every student who participated was risking their entire future: a place at this school meant automatic admission to the best universities in the country and was the key to a bright career. (The leader of the strike was actually expelled, although he's now an executive at Goldman Sachs, close to Central Park—good karma!)

This expression of support made a huge impact on Tanya, and it added a second layer to her first principle of doing things without permission: do them with the help and support of others. Every accomplishment that Tanya has achieved is aligned with that approach to life: she will challenge every preconceived approach to a problem, and surround herself with other people who can help her fix it.

Tanya finished high school in Leningrad, and then she moved with her family to Israel, where she joined the Hebrew University.

Sick and tired of being told what she could and could not do as either a Jew or a woman, Tanya was hungry to try new things. She discovered computers, and graduated with a double major in mathematics and computer science. She then joined the university's Department of Ecology, Evolution and Behavior, and started playing with the idea of applying computer science to ecology—computational ecology.

Tanya quickly started to see things that could be done better. The methods used to study ecology were based on stochastic simulations, where an experiment is run many times with slightly different random variables. In computational ecology, this technique can help predict the impact of an action (such as building a road) on the population of a species, or determine the best repopulation approach for an endangered ecosystem. However, these methods have many limitations.

Tanya decided to apply a different approach to ecology, based on graph algorithms. She moved to the US to continue her work with other experts in the field, and applied it successfully in many areas (such as breeding programs, epidemiology, and animal social interactions).

During that journey she met many new people and was exposed to new problems, and this combination motivated her. One of the people she met was Dr. Dan Rubenstein, one of the foremost zebra experts in the world, who had dedicated his career to the study and protection of the endangered Grevy's zebra.

Dr. Rubenstein was modeling how changes in land use by humans affected zebras' behavior, migration movements, and ultimately population stability. When Tanya met him at Princeton, they had an immediate connection. But in their discussions, Tanya saw again that something was fundamentally broken in the system. Dr. Rubenstein's research relied on archaic methods to capture data. Every day, a collaborator in Kenya had to manually observe and label the zebras in their habitat—a solution that doesn't scale to global efforts at species conservation.

Populations of mammals, birds, fish, reptiles, and amphibians have declined by 60% on average in the past 50 years, and we don't even have the basic data to understand why it is happening or how to fix it. Elephant populations are estimated globally based on very limited data from some parts of Africa. For polar bears, also classified as a vulnerable species, we're lacking the basic data to allow us to even guess at population growth or decline. Estimates of the global population of whale sharks range from 27,000 to 179,000, a level of inaccuracy that severely impacts our ability to understand the problems they face and try to correct them.

Tanya traveled to Kenya to see the zebra observation process in person. Two minutes after she'd begun observing the painfully manual process, Tanya was determined to fix it. Twenty minutes in, she bet with a colleague that she could bring that process down to two clicks.

It took her several years to win that bet, though. Lacking an AI computer vision background herself, she partnered with a student to craft a solution. The goal was to automate the manual and specialized process used to answer the three main questions in species observation: where, when, and who. The first two could be easily answered with GPS-enabled cameras or smartphones, but for the last one they required an AI breakthrough. Could AI identify not only the species, but also an individual within that species?

The answer was yes. Just like the barcodes on your groceries, each zebra has a unique pattern that can be associated with the individual. With just two clicks, a scientist could identify the specific individuals in a picture and create the equivalent of a Facebook "friends list" for zebras.

In January 2016, Tanya helped organize "The Great Grevy's Rally," a crowdsourced event in which regular people such as local community members and students took part. In just two days they took more than 40,000 pictures, and they were able to compile the most accurate and broadest catalog of zebras in history—so accurate that it has been used since then as the official census.

From then on, the progression seemed natural. What if we expand the observation process to every species on the planet, thought Tanya? What if we democratize that observation to every person, making all humans citizen scientists?

To make that vision a reality, Tanya had to work with many more amazing people: a professor in Troy, New York, who was working with his students on a generalized method to identify individuals in any species; an architect from Dell who dedicated his spare time to creating a catalog for whale shark sightings; and a scientist from NASA whose research on pattern matching for constellations was applicable to spot matching in animals.

When Tanya reflects on this journey, what moves her most is not her personal accomplishments. Just as she cherishes the memory of her high school classmates uniting and going on strike for her, what she values the most in her career is how all these people came together to help her achieve her vision.

That vision is a reality today, and it's called Wild Me (*https://oreil.ly/AIO_4a-3*). Wild Me is a nonprofit organization focused on combating extinction with citizen science and artificial intelligence. At its core, Wild Me leverages the years of work put in by many different people to empower every person on the planet to become a citizen scientist. Using AI, Wild Me can process pictures and videos on social media to scale species observation and provide the data researchers need to fight extinction. Every day, Wild Me crawls social sites like YouTube to find sightings and uses AI to identify the when, where, and who for each of them. That metadata is uploaded to an open data platform called Wildbook, which researchers can use to understand the population shifts, migration patterns, or social graphs of animals like whale sharks, whales, manta rays, or turtles.

Tanya and Wild Me represent the next big frontier for AI. The ultimate potential of AI will be realized when every person is empowered with it. AI can democratize tasks that previously required deep expertise. With that approach, domain experts can be scaled globally, increasing their impact and allowing them to focus on a higher level of abstraction. Just as Wild Me enables ecologists to focus on pure research for species conservation instead of gathering data, in health care this technology will help doctors scale to bring medical diagnosis capabilities to every area in the world, and in agriculture it will enable farmers to leverage AI to optimize their crops.

Similarly, in business, AI will truly transform your organization when it goes beyond the realm of the technical and business units, empowering every employee to become a citizen data scientist.

## 4

The People Transformation: Bringing AI to Every Employee

We've explored the first two stages of the transition to an AI organization: transforming our technical departments, bringing AI to every application, then expanding to the business units, bringing AI to every process. But the ultimate realization of the AI organization comes when we go beyond those two steps and bring AI to every employee. Only when every employee is empowered with AI, only when every task performed by every person in the organization has been transformed with AI, can we finally say we have fully become an AI organization.

Think about other technology revolutions and how they went through the same process. Computers initially transformed the business processes in an organization, but the democratization of PCs for employees enabled a deeper transformation, in which every task performed by the employees was augmented or redefined with a computer. The same thing happened with the internet: it allowed departments and employees to consume services directly from technology providers for specific tasks such as project planning, collaboration, or digital marketing. Mobile devices have also ended up being part of the employee toolset, transforming the IT landscape with the concept of Bring Your Own Device (BYOD). When the technology is democratized for every employee, every task they perform can be rethought entirely—and the AI transformation will be no different.

The Birth of the Citizen Data Scientist

A wave of AI democratization in the enterprise is coming. Departments and smaller teams will be empowered to define their own priorities, and the employees themselves will be able to create the AI needed to implement their own solutions. Easy-to-use tools and building blocks will enable a new breed of data scientist—the *citizen data scientist*.

As an organization, you should provide the right environment to empower these new citizen data scientists. The demand for AI in the enterprise will be impossible to meet with traditional technical roles like data scientists and developers. Only empowered business users will be able to fill that gap. For that to happen, there are three primary requirements:

Democratization of knowledge
> There's no AI without data, so the first step in democratizing AI is to democratize the access to the data in your organization, turning data into knowledge that is easy to consume.

Democratization of AI consumption
> After the employees can get access to relevant knowledge in your organization, they need to be able to apply AI on top of it. This can be achieved by providing access to a broad set of prebuilt AI models.

Democratization of AI creation
> The ultimate realization of the citizen data scientist is the ability to create their own AI models with tools adapted to their expertise.

The technologies behind each of these concepts are still emerging and evolving very quickly. For this reason, it is important to take a gradual approach to each of these steps and evolve your approach in tandem with the technology. Let's explore how to do that.

Democratization of Knowledge

A big chunk of the work done by a data scientist is understanding, consolidating, and preparing data. Unfortunately most enterprises have complex data estates, in which data is disseminated across the entire organization in disconnected siloes; it may be unstructured and chaotic, with multiple storage types used.

Nontechnical employees cannot deal with this complexity. To foster citizen data scientists, we first need to provide a data foundation that they can use. The resulting artifact is usually referred as *knowledge*, and it has the following properties:

Knowledge is structured
It contains entities, attributes, and relationships forming a graph. Compared with the raw form of data, knowledge is easy to navigate.

Knowledge is semantic
Every entity, attribute, or relationship is clearly defined. Knowledge can be understood by the user.

Knowledge is consolidated
The information it contains is semantically integrated from different data sources; for example, the "customer" entity could come from multiple different data assets across the organization.

Take search engines as an example. If you search Google or Bing for a common entity like a movie or a person, you will get not only the traditional list of blue links, but also an entity on the right containing the knowledge equivalent of those results (Figure 4-1). In the case of a movie the entity is highly structured, and it will include attributes and relationships with clear semantics (e.g., year, cast, and director). This knowledge is the result of consolidating unstructured and sometimes chaotic information from multiple sources. In Bing, the technology powering this knowledge creation is called Bing Satori; it crawls billions of pages to extract the relevant semantic entities and their attributes, consolidating the data it gathers into a knowledge graph that is displayed.

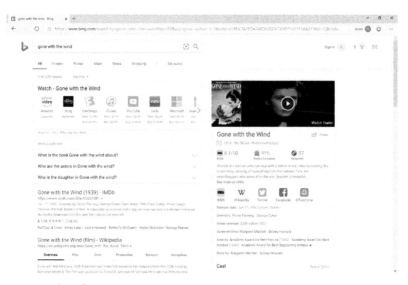

Figure 4-1. Searching for a movie on Bing

We will explore strategies for managing your data estate in Chapter 6, including how to consolidate your data into knowledge that can be consumed by your employees. Once you have that knowledge, no matter how you created it, the next step is to expose it to your employees. A good principle is to expose it through the tools they already use. For example, in the case of Bing Satori, you can also get access to that data from Office. If you want to see this in action you just need to write a list of company names in Excel and use the option Data Types→Stocks, available in the latest versions of Office. The data will automatically be converted into semantic knowledge drawn from Bing Satori, with options to add additional attributes such as number of employees or stock value (Figure 4-2).

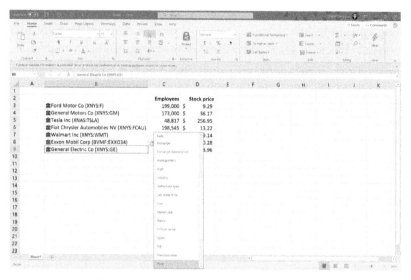

Figure 4-2. Bringing world knowledge to Excel

The same approach can be taken for your internal organizational knowledge: employees can get access to relevant consolidated knowledge about products, parts, customers, or any other relevant business information directly from the tools they use in their everyday work.

Conversational agents are also a very common way of surfacing this knowledge. As mentioned previously, conversational agents that rely on knowledge can provide a richer experience to the user. Connecting internal conversational agents to the underlying knowledge in the organization will make them much richer and more useful for employees. Suddenly, the users will be able not only to provide commands to the agent, but also to ask questions in natural language that are answered based on the knowledge base across the organization.

Democratization of AI Consumption

The next step for empowering employees to become citizen data scientists is to enable them to apply AI on top of the available knowledge. If the AI models in the organization are available for any employee to use and easy to apply to that knowledge, employees will all be free to augment their reasoning with AI. AI is now not constrained to specific applications or processes, but can be used for all the decisions made in the organization.

A good example of this approach is Excel's integration with Azure Machine Learning. As your technical teams develop AI models in Azure, they are automatically made available in Excel. Excel users in your organization can then discover the repository of models published internally and apply them to their data in Excel. That data can come from the unified knowledge in the organization, or can be provided directly by the user (also referred to as Bring Your Own Data). The resulting scenarios can be extremely powerful. Users can now apply AI to day-to-day tasks that previously were performed manually: for example, a sales manager could predict which opportunities their team is likely to close successfully, or a financial sales consultant could identify the customers most likely to purchase a new product.

The AI models can also come from a third-party provider. For example, Power BI provides access to the same prebuilt models available in Azure, enabling its users to easily apply complex AI models like sentiment analysis or image classification to their reports without requiring the technical team in the organization to develop them. For example, a marketer could add sentiment analysis in a social media report, or an insurance employee could apply an image recognition model to the pictures of an accident report.

Democratization of AI Creation

The ultimate realization of the concept of the citizen data scientist is the ability not only to consume preexisting models, but also to *create* new models. This idea may sound crazy. AI model development can appear very complex, and out of the reach of nontechnical users. In fact, it is—creating an AI model from scratch, especially a state-of-the-art one, can be a daunting experience for all but the most experienced data scientists.

However, there are many ways to democratize AI. Although data scientists and developers will still be needed to create more complex and customized models, it's possible for citizen data scientists to implement a significant number of AI solutions by themselves. Gartner (*https://oreil.ly/AIO_4-1*) estimates than 40% of data science tasks will be automated in the near future, enabling citizen data scientists. There are many technologies aimed at facilitating this change, some of them already available in the market and others on which very promising progress is being made.

One of the most common approaches for this democratization of AI creation is *transfer learning*. Transfer learning allows AI models to be customized after they are trained. A data scientist can create the initial model and train it, and another user can customize it for their own scenario without requiring technical skills. Vision is one of the most popular areas in which to apply these techniques. Services like Azure Custom Vision and Google AutoML Vision allow the creation of image classification or object detection models just by uploading a few pictures of the different objects in your scenario. Under the hood, the system is reusing a deep learning model that was created in advance and applying transfer learning to customize that model for your domain. Using this technique you can create a model to identify safety hazards in your factory, or items in your retail store, or whatever else might be appropriate in your industry—all without any deep learning or data science knowledge.

Automated machine learning is another promising approach. Just as transfer learning enables any user to customize an existing model with their own data, automated machine learning enables the user to create net-new models from scratch. AutoML techniques take a dataset as an input and automatically find the best machine learning algorithm, parameters, and data transformations to produce the desired outcome. This process usually involves the data scientist carefully trying multiple combinations, based on their experience. AutoML has the potential to revolutionize machine learning by making it more productive for data scientists and more approachable for nontechnical employees. Microsoft Research has published several papers on this topic, one of them describing a breakthrough (*https://oreil.ly/AIO_4-2*) that is available today in Azure Machine Learning (*https://oreil.ly/AIO_4-3*) and the Power Platform, including PowerBI (*https://oreil.ly/AIO_4-4*) and PowerApps (*https://oreil.ly/AIO_4-5*). With this technology, data scientists can be more productive and business users can create their own state-of-the-art models in just a few clicks.

Graphical tools can also simplify the development of machine learning models, making it more accessible to nontechnical users. With this option, the user can create a model instead of customizing an existing one, although some level of familiarity with machine learning is still required. Azure Machine Learning Studio is an example of this approach: users can create machine learning models by dragging, dropping, and connecting elements in a design surface. Promising technologies in incubation such as Lobe (*https://oreil.ly/AIO_4-6*) are bringing this concept to more complex scenarios, like deep learning.

Another interesting area of research with the potential to democratize AI creation is the concept of *machine teaching*. At its core, machine learning relies on providing a massive quantity of training inputs and outputs and finding the right algorithm to mimic the transformation. Machine teaching focuses instead on decomposing the problem into smaller pieces that the machine can be trained on individually. It's similar to the way humans teach other humans, such as children. For example, as I write this book my wife and I are in the process of teaching our daughter Angela how to brush her teeth. A machine learning developer would give her a thousand YouTube videos of kids brushing their teeth, hoping she would learn from these. A reinforcement learning developer would give her a brush, some toothpaste, and a cup and leave her by herself to play with the three. When she happened to brush her teeth correctly, they would give her some candy. In addition to the paradox of using candy as a reward for a child brushing their teeth correctly, that approach would require a lot of experimentation and probably take a very long time. A responsible father like myself would instead take the machine teaching approach, decomposing the problem into smaller pieces (put some toothpaste on the brush, brush the front teeth, brush the back teeth, pour some water in the glass, rinse your mouth, clean the brush and cup), and then teach each step separately, using my own knowledge.

With this approach, the teacher makes the entire process much easier to learn. Machine teaching systems focus on enabling the teacher to transfer their knowledge to the machine through decomposition, generalization, and examples, instead of applying brute force with a huge amount of data or experiments. Although it is still a new concept in the AI space, there are several examples of technologies using this approach today. For example, the language-understanding service in Azure (LUIS) allows users to define intents and entities from plain language using a machine teaching approach, and Bonsai (*https://oreil.ly/AIO_4-7*), a technology recently acquired by Microsoft, uses a machine teaching approach to enable business users to train autonomous systems such as manufacturing robots, power mills, or oil drills.

AI Democratization Scenarios

When every employee is empowered to create AI solutions and apply them to their own data, the kinds of business transformations we saw earlier can be done independently at the department or even the individual level. Just as they create Access applications, Excel macros, or SharePoint websites, self-service AI will enable power users in every department to create their own AI.

Often, these users will leverage AI models created by a central technical department or a third-party provider, applying them to their own departmental data—imagine branch offices or departments applying algorithms for product recommendation, lead scoring, or customer feedback analysis to their own regional data.

In other cases, these power users could even create their own AI solutions from scratch. AutoML or easy-to-use graphical tools can enable employees to create custom models for customer churn, sales forecasting, or cold calling. Decision-making processes that were previously supported by departmental self-service business intelligence (BI) tools, dashboards, or spreadsheets can now also be supported by self-service AI.

And at the individual level, employees can automate some of their more repetitive tasks with AI. Task automation, which is traditionally addressed with workflow tools, can be greatly simplified with AI. Robotic Process Automation (RPA) automates individual and team processes by just observing the steps performed by a user as they interact with legacy applications. Instead of learning a programming language or a workflow tool, the user can perform the actions for the machine to learn, and the machine can then can generalize these steps and apply them to any case in a fraction of the time needed by a user. For processes dealing with multiple different legacy applications with a lot of manual data entry, RPA technologies can have a massive impact on employee productivity.

Managing Shadow AI

The empowerment of every department and every employee in an organization to create AI can have an unintended effect: as these self-service projects proliferate, you could wind up with hundreds or thousands of siloed and unmanaged AI solutions. Without management by a central function in the company, the result can be a mess of noncompliant, unsecured, and unreliable AI systems.

The good news is that most organizations are already learning how to deal with this issue in the IT domain. Known as *Shadow IT*, the use by employees of applications and infrastructure that are not under the control of an organization's IT department is becoming more widely understood and addressed. Many organizations are working to put solutions in place to enable individuals in every department to bring their own devices to the workplace and to create their own document repositories, applications, dashboards and more, while keeping control over things like security, access, reliability, backups, and privacy.

With AI coming into the hands of every employee, a similar concept known as *Shadow AI* is emerging. Just like Shadow IT, Shadow AI is a powerful force for enabling innovation at the department and the individual level, but it is not without risk.

Therefore, in addition to providing the tools to empower every employee with AI, you'll need to think about providing an environment to manage and control the resulting AI projects—in other words, you'll need to implement an effective Shadow AI strategy. At the very least, this environment should manage the same aspects managed by a Shadow IT policy. Concerns to address include the following:

Access control
> Manage who has access to the models, data, and outcomes of the AI solutions, and ensure access can be revoked at any moment (for example, when an employee leaves the company).

Monitoring
> Track the health and usage of every AI solution, including accuracy metrics (especially those relevant to identifying changes in the data that may impact the model's performance).

Deployment
> Manage the distribution and versioning of all AI solutions, including traceability back to the development process of the model.

Reliability
> Assure the availability of these solutions with automatic scaling and failover.

Security
> Enforce security controls to avoid external attacks or data breaches, including techniques such as encryption and security threat identification.

AI has also unique requirements and challenges that are not present in Shadow IT. AI is more than just a technology; it's a whole new approach to applications, business, and people that requires a cultural shift in the organization. In the next chapters, we will cover the cultural aspects of an AI organization, but before that, let's learn the story of how one person changed the culture of a company with almost 100 years of history.

AI Hero: Chema

Chema (*https://oreil.ly/AIO_5a-1*) knows well the importance of transforming a company's culture to embrace AI. He's chief data officer at Telefónica, one the largest telecommunications companies in the world: it's ranked third in its category on the list of World's Most Admired Companies by Fortune (*https://oreil.ly/AIO_5a-2*), and Morgan Stanley (*https://oreil.ly/AIO_5a-3*) has described it as the European leader in digital transformation. Innovation is the primary factor driving those recognitions—which is a huge achievement considering Telefónica is almost one hundred years old.

How does a company with so much baggage successfully transform itself? José María Álvarez-Pallete, chairman and CEO of Telefónica, knew that such a massive endeavor needed to be led by a person dramatically different from the typical executive. He found that person in Chema. You will spot him easily in any official corporate picture: he's the one wearing a ski hat and a t-shirt depicting one of his favorite comic book superheroes.

Chema grew up in a working-class neighborhood in Móstoles, a suburb of Madrid. His father worked as a construction painter for a very modest salary; Chema didn't stay in a hotel or fly on a plane until he was well into his twenties, and from a young age he had to balance school with helping his father at work.

It was while he was working on a construction site with his father that Chema realized he wanted something different. His mother was always telling him that he should pursue a better life working in an office. She also often told her son that he was no different from any rich person and that anything can be learned with enough effort.

So Chema decided to follow her advice, and set his sights on studying computer science. He'd known he liked computers since he watched *Tron* at the age of eight: in that movie, programs inside computers idolize software developers because they are their creators. While most kids in Spain dreamed of being a soccer star, Chema dreamed of being a developer—although given that no one in his family had ever gone to college, being a soccer star actually sounded like a more realistic option!

Chema did make it to college, earning a bachelor's degree in computer science. One day, while he was chatting with a friend in a bar, they decided to create a business. They picked the name—Informática 64—and designed the logo right there, on a napkin. (That wouldn't be the last important napkin in Chema's career, as weird as that may sound.) They rented a modest office, painted it themselves, and decorated it with furniture they'd picked out of a dumpster.

"Growth hacking" takes on a new meaning when you have no money. Every Friday they would cold-call potential customers, trying to sell them anything they might be interested in: from application development to IT troubleshooting, networking, or training services. They learned quickly and failed fast, and before they'd even noticed they had 40 employees.

You wouldn't find Chema in the office managing the company, though. He considered himself a "road warrior," preferring instead to present at conferences all over the country on his favorite topic: security. Determined not to let success be a blocker that stopped him from learning, he went on to earn a master's degree and then a doctorate, all while working.

I was fortunate to meet Chema during that time. We collaborated at many events targeting developers and enterprises, but I would also find him at random events at small universities in the middle of nowhere. His motivation was to inspire students and show them the amazing world they had open to them, if they just tried hard enough. Just like his mother had with him, Chema wanted to convince those students that anything can be learned and that the seeming limits to their reality could be moved.

His focus led to him becoming a renowned international expert on security. He has written several books, published dozens of articles, and presented at the most prestigious hacking conferences in the world, like DEF CON and BlackHat. He was recently identified as a top inspirational figure for Spanish teenagers, alongside people like Leo Messi and Rafael Nadal, and he is a regular guest on Spanish TV shows.

Chema's unique personality didn't change when his company—the one that started with a sketch drawn on a napkin—was acquired by Telefónica. With the acquisition, he became the chairman of ElevenPaths, the new security services branch of Telefónica, and he was later appointed chief data officer and made a member of the executive committee. He kept on wearing his signature t-shirts and ski hat, and is often spotted riding his skateboard around Telefónica's corporate campus.

That image is more than just a sign of openness in Telefónica. It is an icon representing the cultural transformation that the company is experiencing. That t-shirt and hat represent the management style of a nimble startup in a basement in Móstoles that couldn't afford to buy furniture, a growth-hacking culture that survives one month at a time.

Chema declared a war on meetings in his organization and instead promoted the culture of the hallway: if you need something, go find your colleague and discuss it. He minimizes meetings as much as possible, encourages a flexible work life, and has created innovation labs, company-wide hackathons, and the group of the Crazy Ideas. They work with deadlines aligned with the company's big moments in time, and they communicate those deadlines as broadly as possible, even externally. Moving the deadlines is not an option—an attempt to recreate the sense of urgency at Chema's original startup. You can see many of these new models of agile collaboration, required for an AI organization, in Chapter 6.

But transforming Telefónica into the most innovative telco in Europe required more than an agile culture. Telefónica, like many companies of its size, had been shaped by multiple acquisitions and international expansions over the past century, which had led to geographical and functional silos that are often nearly impossible to break.

The first functional silo, referred to as the "first platform," dates back to the very beginnings of the company in the 1920s. If you want to see those beginnings for yourself, you can watch the Netflix TV show *The Cable Girls*: the main characters in that show work as switchboard operators at Telefónica, with their primary task being to physically route the phone calls by inserting plugs in a switchboard.

That profession disappeared with the creation first of automatic telephone offices, and then digital ones. This digitalization also enabled the creation of a management platform on top of the existing one—the "second platform." This platform added management functions such as network configuration, provisioning, and inventory, as well as business operations such as orders and billing.

On top of this the "third platform" was then added: digital content and services. With the eruption of large internet companies also providing communications and all sorts of other services, the differentiation battle required telcos to begin providing unique services like video content, security, IoT connectivity, and more.

Managing these three platforms, multiplied by each subsidiary and branch, represents a huge challenge for any CDO. Chema calls his approach to this challenge "the daisy strategy."

In a sketch that he once again drew on a napkin (this time in a Thai restaurant), he envisaged a central node or disc (Telefónica Corp) connected to a ring of petals (the subsidiaries). Each petal had a series of private data stores, each of them associated with a platform. The petals were then connected with a common schema (called the Unified Reference Model, or URM) to the central node.

That strategy allowed each subsidiary to remain independent, a critical requirement for keeping them agile and compliant with local data privacy regulations. However, because they were all using the same schema, a new platform was able to emerge spanning all the silos and legacy platforms in Telefónica: the "fourth platform."

The fourth platform consolidates the information contained in the other three across all subsidiaries and branches, and uses all that unified knowledge to add intelligence. This was the technological capacity needed by Telefónica to provide a solid foundation for its AI transformation. (You can read about different approaches to creating the equivalent data strategy in your organization in Chapter 6.)

Implementing a transformation like this is challenging and requires buy-in from every business unit and subsidiary involved—which can take a titanic effort when their goals are usually focused on short-term business results.

Chema addressed this issue with two strategies. First, instead of forcing subsidiaries to migrate to a centralized data storage, he allowed them to keep their data systems, to decide on their evolution, and to maintain full ownership of the operations.

Second, he motivated the teams to adhere to the common contract URM. The central team created multiple out-of-the-box AI solutions that helped local teams to transform their business processes. These solutions were called *gems* and included capabilities such as next best action and product recommendation. Because these gems were built on top of the common schema, subsidiaries had a motivation to implement it so they could leverage these solutions.

The results of this approach were outstanding. Today, Telefónica has normalized data and standard APIs across most of its subsidiaries and units. The initial few gems to bootstrap data estate consolidation have expanded to include more than 60 solutions that have transformed processes across the sales, marketing, customer service, and network operation functions in use cases such as network planning, failure prediction, credit scoring, smart marketing, and virtual support agents.

The star of these solutions is Aura, Telefónica's own digital assistant. Aura builds on top of all the consolidated data provided by the fourth platform in a conversational AI interface available to every customer through multiple channels such as mobile, web, Facebook Messenger, and digital assistants like Google Assistant and Cortana.

But the most iconic implementation of Aura is a physical device called Movistar Home. Movistar Home is powered by AI, and it replaces the oldest device in any telecommunications company: the landline telephone. It can be used not only to make phone calls but also to control all the services provided by Telefónica, such as TV, video calling, and home automation.

Chema still thinks this is just the beginning of the journey. You will find him at public conferences and universities talking about the next big goals in his journey, with the same contagious passion he had when he was in that office he painted himself—and with the same ski hat and the same t-shirt, representing the level of cultural change needed to embrace an AI transformation.

In the following chapters you will learn about the cultural change required by the transition to an AI organization. We'll explore the four core aspects of this change, and the mechanisms to drive it:

The culture of collaboration
> AI requires entirely new approaches that go beyond teams and processes. We will explore the main implications of the increased collaboration between teams and the different organizational approaches that can help make it happen.

The culture of data
> AI relies heavily on data. Without a strong data strategy your company won't be able to have a successful AI strategy. We will cover the typical challenges found in the enterprise data estate, and how to evolve it to make it AI-ready.

The culture of talent
> AI is a completely different paradigm and requires new abilities. We will identify these abilities and the best approaches to upskill your technical departments, business units, and employees to get them.

The culture of ethics

AI brings unique challenges to an organization not only in areas such as privacy and reliability, but also with regard to more complex ethical concerns such as fairness and transparency. We will cover those challenges in detail and discuss approaches and techniques to address them from the beginning.

## 5

The Culture of Collaboration: Organizing Teams

Imagine that your company is a person. What adjectives do you think your customers would use to describe its personality? That's your company's brand perception. What adjectives do you think the employees would use to describe it? That's your culture.

The company culture is the true personality of your organization. It influences how it behaves, what it does, and the way it works. It is anchored on shared assumptions by employees, which heavily guide what they do and how they do it. Any plan, any activity, any initiative that is not aligned with that personality feels unnatural and doesn't stick.

Without a culture aligned with AI, any attempt at embracing it will also feel against the grain and won't stick, either. You can target a few use cases and even be successful in some of them, but you won't be able to truly transform your organization with AI, any more than I could transform myself into a dancer by memorizing a couple of dance moves—it's just not who I am or what I've been preparing for.

Fortunately, unlike me, company culture can be changed. It's the result of many factors that we can act on: the way the company is organized, the leadership style, the communication strategy, talent management, training, rewards... these are all aspects we can control that help shape the culture of the organization. This chapter will focus on one important factor: the team structure and collaboration model.

From Projects to Products to Platform

Traditionally, enterprise IT has been managed as a set of individual projects. It is very tempting to apply the same model to AI—you can identify the high-priority use cases, kick off a project for each of them, and assign them people, goals, and plans. That approach sounds practical and easy to manage, but it will actually undermine your broader vision to transform the organization with AI.

Project-based IT management is being replaced in many organizations by *product*-based IT management. The concept is simple: instead of managing the IT services as individual projects that have a beginning and an end, we approach them as products that are in continuous evolution. A product management strategy focuses more on the needs of the user, continuously providing value to better serve those needs. A project-based approach focuses more on the tasks, and successfully delivering the results. After we deliver those results, we move on to the next project.

Building a house is a great example of project-based management. You can design the house in great detail before you even start to build it, and you can plan every step in the construction with very high accuracy. After the house is built, you move on to the next one.

Building software is very different. It is difficult to design it at a high level of detail in advance, and it is even more difficult to plan every step in its construction. To make matters more interesting, the needs will be changing all the time, even after it's delivered. The equivalent in the house construction example would be getting a request from the homeowner to add one more bedroom after the house is built, or to change the entire orientation of the house, or (I'm sure IT readers will be able to relate) to add 10 more floors to a single-floor house.

AI is even more challenging. In such an emerging field, it's impossible to perfectly plan every step along the way, and it's even difficult to guarantee that a particular outcome will ever be achieved.

AI scenarios are in continuous evolution. As data changes, the AI on top of it must change too. A project-based mindset for AI would have bad consequences; projects wouldn't meet the initial expectations and would soon be rendered obsolete by changes in the requirements or the underlying data.

In a sense, even a product-based management strategy is not sufficient for the deep transformation required by AI. Recall that the different parts of an AI organization are interconnected. As you transform your technical departments, they have to serve the business units. As you transform the business units, they have to serve the employees. The resulting structure looks more like a platform, as shown in Figure 5-1.

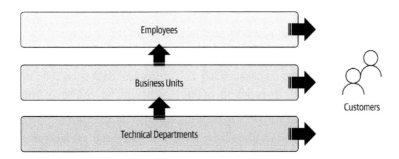

Figure 5-1. Platform structure in an AI organization

In platform-based management, not only you should consider the final users of your products, but every product should also serve as the foundation for other products in your organization.

For technical departments, this means that in addition to bringing AI to the applications, they should also provide core AI services to the business units. For business units, this means that as they transform their business processes with AI, they should also enable business users to create and apply AI solutions on top of them.

Microsoft is an extreme example of a platform-centric company. Our product portfolio is layered into tiers, from the core platform services in Azure to the business services in Dynamics 365 to the user services in Microsoft 365. Each layer is its own entity, and is designed to serve the layer on top of it.

In the platform approach, you should think of every product as having two audiences: the final users, and other products in the company. At Microsoft, we refer to that concept as *first party equals third party* (1P = 3P): the idea is that every product we develop for a particular business should also be considered as a platform for customers. The other way around is also true—every service we develop in the platform should consider the other businesses as their customers. This requires a shift in mindset:

- Product definition should be done not only with the needs of the team leading the product in mind, but as part of a much broader exercise including other teams in the company.

- Every product should be designed with composability in mind and be fully accessible to others. Different products should be able to integrate.

- Common services and assets such as identity and data should be unified as much as possible in order to make it possible for multiple products to come together.

- Duplicated capabilities should be identified early and avoided as much as possible.

- Components such as AI models should be reused across all layers in the organization and easily discoverable through mechanisms like repositories.

Architecting Teams for a Platform Approach: MLOps

A project-based approach is a dream come true for management. You have full flexibility to move people between projects, optimizing resource utilization and increasing specialization. Teams can be organized by function (developers, data scientists, program managers, etc.), and a resource manager can assign the right people to the right project in real time.

It's a pity that doesn't work for AI. The resulting organizational model would try to build AI like a house. Business owners would create the specifications and plan for an entire project. After spending weeks defining this plan they would hand it over to the technical team, who would try to execute it. But without close involvement from the business, the project team would have to make various implementation decisions along the way, and the resulting outcome might not be valuable for the business anymore. Even if it were, the project would stall at some point when the business requirements or the data underneath changed.

Rather than organizing teams by functions, a much more appropriate way of tackling this problem is by creating agile, autonomous teams, with the business involved throughout the whole process. With this approach, all the roles required to manage the product end-to-end are represented in each team: developers, data scientists, product managers, and whatever else is required for the product.

Because they operate autonomously, the teams are much more agile and better able (and motivated) to deliver a successful product.

Teams structured like this and driven by agile methodologies are already being used by almost every software company on the planet, including Microsoft. We even changed our office configuration to support this model, creating common areas where these multidisciplinary teams could work together. In a sense, each of these teams operates like a small startup inside a big corporation. They are highly autonomous, motivated, and driven by the success of the final product rather than by individual goals.

A good test to assess whether your organization is working with this model is the following: ask a data scientist in your company what they are paid for. Very likely, they will say something along the lines of "creating high-quality models" or "delivering AI solutions on time." If that's the case, your organization is probably not functioning in agile, autonomous teams.

All the members of an autonomous team should feel responsible for the business outcomes of the product they are working on. Every member of the team should reply to the question of what they're paid for with the business metrics initially defined for that product, be they revenue, customer satisfaction, or anything else (see Chapter 3).

These teams not only include the product definition and product development components, but also the operations component. *DevOps* (or the equivalent for AI, usually referred to as *MLOps*) is an approach that brings operations and development together. A key aspect of it is continuous deployment, which allows the team to continuously deliver value from development to production, instead of waiting days or weeks for a different team to do so.

When you develop a product this way, you can bring one more stakeholder into the product development process: the user. DevOps is the critical piece that makes these usually autonomous stakeholders work in cooperation with product development. It allows you to include all your constituents in the development process, to make sure what's being built is what the user actually wants.

Who are the constituents? In a platform approach, we need to include several of them:

Business users

> The middle tier of the platform. In the case of a technical team, the business units should be part of it and should be involved in all stages of product development.

Final users

Employees for internal products or, for external-facing products, real customers. An absolute must-have for agile development is to involve the end user in the product as soon as possible to get early feedback.

Other products in the company

This allows you to ensure the product is aligned with the rest of the platform. It means that you will avoid duplicating work or creating different products that don't integrate or compose correctly.

When you include these constituents throughout the entire development cycle, you make sure technology and business outcomes are always in sync and don't diverge during the development process. You can continuously track your progress with regard to the strategy you defined initially and compare it to the goals you set.

THE AGILE LOOP OF MLOPS

For this to happen you need to be able to capture as much information as you can from the system in production, so the loop is closed. Telemetry is one the most foundational components of DevOps. When we bring the user into the development process itself, we need to use telemetry to understand how the system is being used. This telemetry can be explicit, like when we directly ask the user about their experience (via survey questions, like/don't like buttons in the interface, feedback options, etc.), and also implicit, with data generated as the product is used (clickthroughs, abandon rates, user flows, and so forth).

When telemetry is heavily used, the product definition can also be driven by data. How existing products are used is an excellent indicator of the users' needs for future products or features. Product managers can use data-driven decisions to complement user research or their own intuition.

After the initial releases, telemetry will also be critical to evolve an AI solution. Model accuracy will degrade over time as conditions change. A monitoring dashboard consolidating all the telemetry data from your AI models is critical in an AI organization, as well as an established process that can react quickly to sudden drops in model performance.

When designing the MLOps solution for your organization, you should also assure traceability. Traceability will help you connect a specific model at a specific time back to the entire product lifecycle. For example, if a model is showing a lack of accuracy or bias in its decisions, you should be able to identify the version of the model, the history of changes, the team members responsible for those changes, and even the data that was used to train the model.

Telemetry will help you identify issues very quickly in your AI system, but traceability will help you identify the causes of those issues, which team members should be able to fix them, the model version and source code to fix, and even the data that was used.

Once the issue is corrected, you still have to deploy the system again to production. MLOps should also manage the continuous integration process. As changes are made to the product, the entire process from packaging the application to deploying it to production can be automated. Approval gates can be set up so updates don't move through the process unless certain automatic or manual validation criteria are met. These can include performance requirements (e.g., compute or memory resources consumed), quality requirements (e.g., accuracy of the model), or even requirements for responsible AI, which you'll learn about in Chapter 8.

With the right MLOps infrastructure in place, the definition/development/operations loop shown in Figure 5-2 can be dramatically accelerated. The result is a product that is developed with the stakeholders (business, users, and other products) closely integrated in the process, and in continuous evolution with telemetry data coming from its real usage.

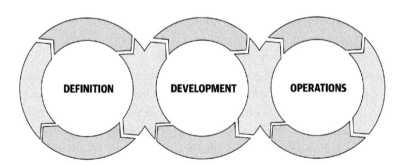

Figure 5-2. MLOps loop

This agile loop and the multidisciplinary nature of the development will be the foundation for how autonomous teams operate in an AI organization:

- *Definition* includes aspects such as the business understanding, experimentation with initial modeling, and data acquisition. It is driven primarily by business stakeholders in close collaboration with developers.

- *Development* is focused on the actual implementation of the solution, including activities such as data preparation, modeling, and training. It is driven primarily by developers and it follows a continuous integration approach in which the solution is incrementally developed and validated.

- *Operations* manages the system in production. It is also fully connected with development through continuous deployment, and provides telemetry back to the development process to help evolve the solution over time.

Services like Azure Machine Learning (*https://oreil.ly/AIO_5-1*) can help your team set up an entire MLOps system like the one described here, taking care of the infrastructure required to implement this agile loop.

Creating an AI Team

Beyond these teams that are operating autonomously in your organization, having a centralized AI-focused team of some sort will be very helpful to bootstrap the initial stages of your AI transformation. It will provide a center of gravity for your organization as well as strong accountability.

However, when creating such a team, you can explore different options for its scope. At the very minimum, this team should be the cross-company virtual leader for the AI transformation. That includes responsibilities like rallying the organization around AI, defining the strategy, identifying and planning the key AI initiatives and products, and evaluating technology solutions. This team should have a strong background and training in AI, and enough business experience and internal connections to apply that expertise to the business.

Beyond leading AI in the organization, a natural progression in scope for this team is to support the rest of the organization with additional functions such as:

AI research
Incubating technologies that can be used by the rest of the teams

AI architecture
> Designing high-level technology components, as well as the interconnections between them

AI production
> Providing core services to support the operations teams

MLOps
> Providing services to the development teams, such as collaboration, security, telemetry, and continuous integration

AI training
> Delivering AI training to the rest of the organization

Providing these functions centrally is usually advisable. The concept of autonomous AI development teams is extremely powerful, but it doesn't scale if you don't complement those teams with supporting functions. Imagine dozens of autonomous teams doing the same foundational research, or creating their own DevOps and production systems. Decentralizing these functions would result in duplicated work and a lack of visibility and control across teams.

Finally, the ultimate level of centralization is for the AI team to host these autonomous development teams themselves. This means that the AI team will also be the one developing solutions, which makes it extremely independent and agile but also brings the risk of a weaker connection to the business. In this situation, you will need especially strong connections between the business units and the centralized team, plus heavy endorsement from the leadership team to make sure the business units are accountable, as well.

WHERE SHOULD THE AI TEAM REPORT TO?

Where to create the AI team is always a tricky decision. In some organizations it makes sense to add these functions to the IT department under the chief information officer (CIO). That can be a fitting arrangement if the IT department is already responsible for developing software or providing the supporting functions for other groups doing software development. In other companies, these functions are consolidated under the chief data officer (CDO). That approach can also make a lot of sense given that the CDO's office is already on point for data and advanced analytics, which have a natural progression to AI. In other cases, these functions are the responsibility of other parts of the organization, such as the chief technical officer's (CTO's) office or the research team. The final decision really depends on your company's situation and aspects like:

- The change management needed. What organization has the closest functions and skills already?

- The existing dynamics in the organization. Is the team already perceived as the leader driving the AI transformation across the business units?

- The technical/business balance. Does the team have enough technical skills, combined with a great connection to the business?

- Resource ownership. Does the team own a good percentage of the resources needed to execute the AI transformation, or will it depend on help from other teams to make it happen?

- Leadership. Does the team's leadership have enough background and expertise to lead this transformation?

Some companies for which there is no clear fit for these functions are opting for creating a new department focused on AI, led by a new C-suite role—the chief AI officer (CAIO). A fresh start with this new department can create the required focus and specialization, which is sometimes difficult to get in existing departments with a lot of baggage.

It's not uncommon to follow hybrid approaches, as well. The IT department can provide the core infrastructure functions such as the production systems and MLOps services, and the CDO's office can provide functions related to data and architecture. Development teams can be expanded from existing data science and application development teams in a central department or the business units. The AI team in that case can be scoped to the leadership role and orchestration across all those different teams, and in extreme cases it can even be relegated to just a virtual team across them.

No matter what approach you take, you will always end up with a new department, team, or virtual team that will become the primary driver of the AI transformation across the entire business. In all cases, this team's success will rely heavily on its level of empowerment and connection to the business—and even a new department led by a fully empowered CAIO will need to battle internal resistance and the inertia of the current business.

That's where the CEO has to step in. Every big transformation requires the company's leadership to provide a clear vision and prioritization. Without the CEO clearly articulating the importance and the vision behind the AI transformation, the internal resistance would likely be impossible to overcome. The entire company needs to understand the reasons for the change and the criticality and extent of it. This can take the form of a simple communication like the famous "Internet Tidal Wave" memo from Bill Gates or the "For the cloud, we're all in" communication from Steve Ballmer, but it's usually much more than that. It's continuously reinforcing the vision in every communication, both internal and external. It's updating the company's vision and mission. It's changing the processes and even the employee compensation. It's bringing the board along on the journey.

Without full buy-in from every business unit and every employee, the goals of the AI team pushing for the AI transformation would be impossible to achieve. The use cases would be the wrong ones for the business. The lack of involvement from the business users would result in products that don't meet the requirements.

Once that leadership endorsement is in place, success will rely on the team's ability to earn the trust of the business. Multidisciplinary, agile teams are usually very helpful in making that happen. Providing continuous value and driving a shared process for prioritization can help avoid misalignment with the business. Business units are usually in the performance zone: they're particularly motivated by short-term revenue generation and cost-saving projects. Because of that, balancing these types of short-term projects with longer-term moonshots is also very helpful in order to have a healthy AI/business partnership.

Only companies with very strong AI-supporting functions as a foundation and full buy-in from the leadership will be able to develop a strong integration with the business and succeed in the journey to becoming an AI organization.

BUILDING VERSUS BUYING

Building your AI products in-house is not an option for many organizations. The skills gap or just the economics may mean it's not feasible to rely only on internal resources.

The decision of whether to build or buy is not all or nothing, though. Many scenarios can be addressed with the existing talent in the organization. For example, most of the examples of bringing AI to applications that you saw in Chapter 3 can be handled by existing application developers, using prebuilt AI services and conversational AI platforms and drawing on the skills they already have. For organizations with existing data science teams, it is also a natural progression to target custom AI scenarios applied to business processes—and business users and analysts who are already doing business intelligence are great candidates for using self-service AI scenarios.

However, you will usually need to complement this strategy, either by acquiring prebuilt software-as-a-service (SaaS) solutions or by outsourcing custom development to third-party vendors. Good candidates are products supporting your horizontal processes, such as sales, marketing, customer service, or HR. The use cases in those processes are relatively common in the industry, and it's often easy to find packaged solutions that provide immediate value.

On the other hand, vertical processes specific to your industry and your company are excellent candidates to develop in-house or in a close partnership with a vendor that can custom-develop the solutions. These vertical processes are usually the ones that differentiate your company from the competition, and you want to put as much attention and customization into them as possible.

In all these approaches, the role of the internal AI team is critical. A strategy involving in-house development, third-party SaaS solutions, and custom-made outsourced products cannot be successful without a strong foundation of supporting functions. The resulting architecture would become unmanageable very quickly, siloed into specific use cases that aren't composable or reusable. All the supporting functions, from data management to MLOps to production to architecture, should be centralized in the company and shared across any built, bought, or outsourced solution.

Once you find the right organizational structure and collaboration model for your team, you can start creating your first AI solutions. But before that, you need to have a foundational data estate that can feed your AI solutions. That is the focus of our next chapter.

## 6

The Culture of Data: Leveraging Your Data Estate

AI relies heavily on data, and it will only be as relevant to your organization as the data you use to train it. No matter what scenario you are targeting, chances are that without relevant data, you won't be successful in delivering an AI solution.

Because data is created everywhere in your organization, it requires everybody to be involved. Your strategy for handling your data estate will need to address not only the technology and governance, but also a cultural change across the company. That data estate includes the operational data in your enterprise applications, such as your CRM or ERP, but it's much broader than that and may include the following:

- Unstructured information coming from the physical world (scanned documents, blueprints, contracts, photographs, videos, etc.)
- Usage data generated in your SoE applications (websites, mobile applications)
- Data coming from your IoT devices (sensors, controllers, etc.)
- Employee-generated data, primarily coming from productivity tools (spreadsheets, emails, meetings, and the like)
- Global and third-party data used to enrich your own data estate

In this chapter you will learn how to bring this vast amount of data together; we'll look at the technologies and different approaches involved, and the cultural change required to make it happen.

Technologies Involved

With such a diverse ecosystem of data from different sources and in different shapes, one of the main challenges in any organization is the dispersion of data. For years, in enterprises around the world, project-driven culture has created hundreds or even thousands of siloed systems. Data just sits in those silos and serves only the original purpose of the application or project for which it was created.

In other cases, with silos designed with a "selfish" mentality, the data is not even created in the first place: if it's not useful for that specific domain the data is not gathered or surfaced, meaning other areas that could reuse that data miss out on a great opportunity (think of legacy systems inside black boxes, or the intelligence latent in departmental Excel spreadsheets).

AI needs a very different approach. To create relevant AI solutions, the data feeding them should be as rich and broad as possible. AI models are much more accurate if they are trained with diverse signals. A sales model for identifying the best next action of a seller will be much more powerful if you use not only the CRM data to train it, but also internal documents or emails, external data about the company, and/or customer engagement data from your website or mobile applications.

For years, companies have tried to consolidate their data estates to solve this problem. Even before AI was such a hot topic, companies needed to create reports based on their business data. A common approach was to build those reports on top of the operational data in the enterprise applications, but there were a few issues with that solution:

- Reports usually needed data from multiple enterprise applications at the same time.

- Users running compute-intensive reports could have a performance impact on critical operational systems.

To resolve these issues, a number of technology solutions emerged over time. Let's take a look at the most popular ones.

OPERATIONAL DATA STORES

A common option for operational reporting is to implement an operational data store (ODS). An ODS consolidates data from multiple structured, transactional systems. It basically creates a read-only copy of the operational data in a different database. This data can be brought in from multiple sources, and in this process it can perform basic operations such as cleaning, connecting entities from different sources, and resolving conflicts.

If you have ODSs in your organization, they are potential candidates for AI training, but they are far from being comprehensive enough. They cover only operational data, usually from only a few data sources and without keeping a history. Therefore, their scope is limited. And even before AI, the ODS approach had a big limitation—as the business requested more powerful reports, the ODS couldn't keep up. Business users wanted dashboards and key performance indicators (KPIs) with more complex aggregations and statistics over the data, which the ODS approach couldn't provide. The answer to that was the data warehouse.

DATA WAREHOUSES

A data warehouse also brings in data from multiple sources in a read-only fashion, but it doesn't use a traditional database to store it. Instead of rows of data, a data warehouse stores the data as dimensions and facts, which greatly simplifies the aggregation of data. For example, a data warehouse can easily get an aggregation of the revenue for a particular product in a particular country and even for a particular year. The result is also referred to as a "data cube," where the axes are the dimensions (in this case product, country, and year) and the content of the cube is the fact (in this case revenue). This structure makes them extremely useful for navigating through aggregations and defining KPIs.

Data warehouses are also great candidates as training sources for AI. They usually integrate data from many operational applications and also include historical data. However, just like ODSs, they are still focused on structured business data.

DATA LAKES

An alternative to data warehouses that companies are embracing at scale is the concept of the data lake. A data lake, just like an ODS or data warehouse, brings in data from multiple sources in the organization; however, the data is stored in its raw format, without any requirements on its structure. Because of this, anything can be stored in a data lake: from structured business data to nonstructured data such as documents, images, emails, or log files.

This quality of data lakes makes them perfect as consolidated data stores for an organization, and they are very popular as sources for training AI models. However, they are more difficult to manage and consume. Because the data is in its raw format, it can be difficult to understand. To make things more interesting, a data lake provides a store with no compute capabilities, so users will also need a distributed computing system such as Apache Spark to actually do something with the data. For these reasons, data lakes are usually limited to data scientists and are not appropriate for consumption by other roles in the organization, at least in their raw format.

KNOWLEDGE GRAPHS

To complement data lakes, organizations are also embracing the concept of knowledge graphs. Knowledge graphs are on the other end of the spectrum from data lakes: they offer semantic information with typed entities, properties, and relationships. From that angle, they are closer to operational business data because the information they store is structured. However, knowledge graphs are created from unstructured data.

An example of a knowledge graph is powering the Bing Satori technology mentioned in Chapter 4. The highly structured results you see when searching for an entity in Bing such as a movie or a person are based on the underlying knowledge graph. This semantic data is coming from the billions of pages crawled by Bing and extracted using AI techniques such as natural language processing.

The power of a knowledge graph in the enterprise is that it can bring together both structured and unstructured data. It is able to understand chaotic data—even contradictory data in some cases—and build a highly semantic graph as a result. If it's able to make sense out of billions of pages on the internet, it can also make sense out of the chaotic data present in any enterprise.

The unstructured data can be documents, like in the case of Bing, but it can also be any other type of content, such as images, audio, or video. With the appropriate AI model it's possible to extract information from scanned contracts, customer forms, photographs, or any other potential data sources that were previously siloed and inaccessible in the organization. Azure provides this concept as part of its cognitive capabilities, also referred to as *knowledge mining*.

Consolidating Your Data Estate: Data Hubs

After that brief crash course on data technologies, hopefully you now understand why consolidating a data estate is so difficult. Operational data stores, data warehouses, data lakes, knowledge graphs—each of these has its own purpose, and it's difficult to standardize on just one. Even if you could, having only one data store for the entire organization is not practical, because different departments or functional areas need the flexibility of their own stores to be agile. Branches or even entire companies in the case of acquisitions will also have their own entire data estates that will need to coexist with the rest.

Instead of attempting to consolidate everything in one data store, many organizations are embracing a more practical approach known as a *data hub*. This architectural pattern is focused on connecting and exposing the existing data sources in an organization—instead of bringing all the data into the same store, a data hub is a hybrid approach that allows you to keep the data in multiple stores, such as data lakes or data warehouses, but centralize the access to and management of that data.

More than a technology, a data hub is a strategy. Instead of consumers of data (such as AI solutions) having to discover and connect with each individual data source, they can have a unified view of the data in the data hub. This hugely simplifies the development of solutions across multiple previously siloed sources.

Because it's more of a strategy than a technology, a data hub is very flexible. You can decide which capabilities you want to centralize and which you want to leave up to each data source. There are three important capabilities to consider. In some cases you will want all of them to be handled by the data hub, and in other cases perhaps none of them:

Data semantics

A data hub can add semantics to unstructured data or unify semantics from disparate structured data sources. This is extremely powerful for data sources such as data lakes that lack structured semantics, and when data is structured but not unified (for example, data sources in different branches or from acquired companies).

Data storage

A data hub can physically copy the data from a data source or just refer to it. In the first case, the consumer of the data won't need to access the original data source. In the second case, the level of complexity is lower because it doesn't have to deal with loading, synchronization, or storage issues.

Data governance

A data hub brings an excellent opportunity to centralize the data governance in an organization. Because all consumers of data will connect through the data hub, you can enforce aspects like security, access control, data quality, privacy, or compliance.

Data-Driven Culture

This may sound great, but all of these beautiful data warehouses, data lakes, and data hubs will do nothing for your organization if they are not complemented with a cultural change.

A data-driven culture should be led from the highest levels of the organization and be infused throughout every team and every employee. It is usually focused on encouraging three core behaviors: generating your own data, sharing high-quality data with others, and leveraging others' data.

The first behavioral change seems obvious. If the data is not created in the first place, there's no way you can have a compelling data estate. Every process, every product, every task should be created in such a way that data is collected along the way. Just as every product should provide telemetry, every process in the company should also be instrumented: back office processes, frontline processes, even processes on edge devices. All of this data will provide an amazing breadth of information that your organization can draw on to redefine these processes with AI.

The second step in fostering a data-driven culture is sharing that data. If data stays siloed in a department, team, or individual, it is difficult for the rest of the organization to do anything with it. Any consolidation approach can work only if every person in the organization embraces it. But that doesn't mean you should just share your team's databases or your individual Excel spreadsheets—it means making the effort to turn it into high-quality data that can be easily consumed by others. With the data hub approach, that means complying with all the requirements it enforces (security, semantics, formats, policies).

The last step, which closes the circle of a data-first culture, is encouraging users to make use of that organizational data estate. In real life, you won't have perfect data just waiting around for you to use it. Using the data that's available will close the feedback cycle that truly enforces quality. When teams and employees make decisions, optimize their activities, or gain insights by using the data estate, not only will they significantly improve those processes, but they will also close the cycle for that data. I personally learned this culture in the Developer Division in Microsoft. Product owners were encouraged, even forced, to use data to support any claim or product-planning decision. This created the motivation to also generate the data in the products they designed, as well as using data from others. This cycle of data creation, sharing, and consumption is the foundation of a data-first culture in any organization.

When all of this happens, the resulting data estate is a gold mine for amazing AI and the foundation for the AI organization. Data scientists can use raw data from across the company to create entirely new approaches to business with custom AI models. Developers can create truly intelligent applications and conversational agents that are connected with the business. And every employee can leverage this powerful source to gain insights, predict outcomes, and even create their own self-service AI solutions.

The importance of a data-first culture became very clear to Julián when he first began working on his project to redefine rare disease diagnosis. Medical records were mostly unusable for training the AI models his non-profit, Foundation 29, was creating. With nobody else making use of their notes, doctors had been trained to take notes for themselves since college. The stereotype of doctors having terrible handwriting is mostly caused by the medical culture of documenting procedures just for their own future consumption. It's the data silo problem to the extreme, because the silo is not the department or the organization, but each individual.

Julián is far from completely solving this problem, but he found that involving doctors in the process and getting their buy-in was critical to encouraging them to generate high-quality data. The AI-driven rare disease diagnosis tool created by Foundation 29 is not perceived as a threat to or an attempt to replace the doctor. In fact, doctors are eager to get access to tools that can allow them to augment their capabilities, be more precise, and spend more time with their patients. The real-time feedback loop with the AI system encouraged them to create more relevant data that produced better results—a great example of the virtuous cycle of a data-driven culture.

Chema at Telefónica experienced a similar problem. In his case, he found that providing gems—those out-of-the-box solutions for subsidiaries—was a great motivator to get them to adopt a common data schema. Telefónica's data hub was primarily focused on enforced semantics, and left the rest decentralized. The central team designed the schema across the entire organization for entities like *customer*, *invoice*, and *package*. Subsidiaries were allowed to continue their operations locally and keep their existing data platforms with no change, but they were encouraged to expose their data using the organization-wide contract.

This approach was amplified with a company-wide readiness initiative to help every employee understand the benefits of a unified data strategy and teach them about the main tools available to help them embrace it. At conferences, Chema still shares one of the videos of this training course. In the video, the presenter talks to the camera as he's building a tower made of LEGO bricks. He explains how the walls of the tower are the data silos in Telefónica. He then puts a floor on top of those pieces, representing the common schema. This floor provides a strong foundation on which amazing things can be built. He goes on to build a really tall tower on top of that common foundation, capping it off with the conversational AI agent Aura, which uses all of the data and AI platforms underneath it.

AI Hero: Cristian

Cristian (*https://oreil.ly/AIO_7a-1*) was a teenager with many passions, but he needed a push to help him enjoy them to the fullest. Oddly, that push came when he was 18 years old and was involved in a car accident that caused full and permanent blindness. When he talks about the accident, you won't hear any complaints. Actually, it's just the opposite. He sees that accident as having created a new opportunity for him to find joy in things he was taking for granted and motivation to pursue those passions.

Cristian was energized by the accident, and saw it as a chance to learn things again and feel that sense of accomplishment that other people usually have just once in their lives. How many of us can remember how amazing it was to learn how to read? You probably weren't even conscious of the world of possibilities that opened up to you in that moment in your life. Cristian was fortunate enough to reexperience that moment when he learned how to read Braille at age 19. He still remembers the sense of accomplishment and his joy at the possibilities that would bring to him, like being able to choose the music he wanted to listen to from his collection of vinyl records.

Learning to read again was just the beginning. Everything that Cristian had liked to do as a teenager was now more exciting because he had to learn it again. Like many of the AI heroes in this book, Cristian also had a personal computer, on which he learned to program (parents of today: think about that for your kids!). In his case Cristian got an Apple II, which he was able to earn by sacrificing a vacation trip.

His blindness only fueled his passion for computers. He learned to program again, with the help of specialized hardware that could make the text-based interface of those times accessible for him. Cristian went from being a mediocre student to wanting to excel at everything that he did. He went to college to study computer science, but even before finishing he felt he needed a new challenge in his learning journey.

He left college and decided to focus on another one of his hobbies from his teenage days: skiing. And he experienced the same joy relearning how to do this as he had for reading, programming, and taking a bus. Again, the learning opportunity ignited a passion to excel. From being a hobbyist skier with sight, he became a multiple-time champion in Spain and Europe and even went to the Paralympics in Japan in 1998.

Cristian kept on working with computers during this adventure. With the birth of graphical user interfaces things became a little more difficult for the blind community: a revolution meant to bring computers to more people was actually a big barrier for the segment of the population with visual disabilities. Again, this only motivated Cristian even more. Not only he did not run away from graphical interfaces, he embraced them and drove change.

Cristian specialized in Windows and Office. He was a trainer and often delivered courses to enterprise employees. I would easily sacrifice my pinky toe to see the faces of those employees when they realized their teacher was blind.

At around that time, Cristian's attention was captured by ONCE (*https://oreil.ly/AIO_7a-2*), a Spanish organization that provided services to blind people. It had its origins during the Spanish civil war, with representatives selling charity lottery tickets that funded the social services provided to the blind. Eventually ONCE diversified its business through the ONCE Business Corporation, with stakes in hotels, services, and food companies. Today, ONCE Group employs more than 136,000 people, 88% of whom are people with disabilities. Its nonprofit arm, the ONCE Foundation, is one of the most impactful organizations in the world for people with disabilities: it works in diverse areas of accessibility, from urban architecture to employment, sports, and digital technologies.

It's in this last area where ONCE and Microsoft's stories come together. In 1997, the companies signed a collaboration agreement to adapt the popular Windows 95 for people with reduced vision. ONCE specialists worked together with Microsoft engineers in Redmond to create what was the most accessible graphical operating system at that time: Windows 98.

By now you probably only remember Windows 98 for its support of Plug and Play and its early demo during which a very young Chris Capossela received the most famous blue screen in history, live on stage with Bill Gates. However, two other notable things happened after that.

First, Chris became chief marketing officer at Microsoft. He's a big advocate of "courageous learning," just like our AI hero Cristian. He will tell you that the only way to grow is to make mistakes and feel uncomfortable, like he did in that demo. He applies that approach to other areas in his life too, like becoming an advocate at Microsoft for diversity and inclusion—a role in which, as a white middle-aged male, he again had to find the courage to feel uncomfortable and learn from it.

Second, thanks to the partnership with ONCE, Windows 98 was the beginning of accessible graphical operating systems. It included many capabilities that were unique at its time, like high contrast, zoom, voice integration, and an accessible internet browser, and played a big role in bringing technology to the low-vision community in the world.

Cristian joined ONCE at around that time, after his skiing adventure. He started in the sports area, helping to bring the same joy he'd experienced to other people with disabilities. Soon enough, he was working in the technology area, and after a few years he became the CIO of ONCE. Since then he has been working very closely with Microsoft and other providers to make sure technology doesn't leave anybody behind. He and his organization work with regulators to make accessibility a requirement for any website or software application, and as CIO he leads the internal IT team at ONCE.

In this journey, Cristian has experienced a fundamental change in technology and its relationship with accessibility. For years, Cristian and ONCE were focused on breaking down barriers between technology and people with disabilities. In a sense, they were doing a *defensive* play: by working with providers and regulators, they were making sure that the advances in new technologies were not limited to just one segment of the population.

A great example of this was the point-of-sale (POS) terminal modernization at ONCE: the organization deployed a fully accessible POS terminal to all its sales points, allowing its blind sellers to make transactions, check for prizes, and void unsold tickets. This new system saved them a daily trip to the central office. By removing a technological barrier, ONCE was able to bring the benefits of the IT transformation to all its employees.

Then, something wonderful started to happen. What previously had been seen as science-fiction technology was becoming a reality. Artificial intelligence was already providing very promising results in the fields of perception and human interaction. When computers can see, hear, and speak, they can remove not only technological barriers, but also barriers in the physical world.

Suddenly there was the potential for technology to take on a huge new role for people with disabilities. What was a defensive play in the past, just trying to make sure they were not excluded from advances in technology, could now turn into an *offensive* play. Artificial intelligence can connect people with disabilities with their environment. It can narrate to blind people what is happening around them, transcribe human voice for deaf people, help nonverbal children on the autism spectrum communicate, automate wheelchairs for people with reduced mobility, and so much more.

Cristian was putting a hundred percent into this opportunity, but believe it or not, he had more to do. After becoming a skiing champion and spending eight years working at ONCE, rising through the ranks to lead the IT team at the company (which by then had more than 100,000 employees), he decided to pursue yet another of his passions from before he'd become blind. Cristian wanted to be a chef.

Like everything else, Cristian also had to relearn how to cook. He still remembers the tears in his eyes when he was able to cook his first grilled cheese sandwich as a blind person. That burnt piece of bread with greasy butter and cheese seemed like the most exquisite delicacy he'd ever eaten.

Some years after that sandwich, while still working at ONCE, Cristian decided to open a restaurant. He was involved in all aspects of the business, including the kitchen. Watching Cristian cook is an amazing experience. The rest of us rely heavily on our sense of sight, which if you think about it shouldn't be the most important for cooking. Cristian uses his senses of smell, taste, touch, and even hearing to prepare wonderful meals that would delight the most demanding chefs in Spain.

After accomplishing this amazing achievement, Cristian realized he couldn't maintain both his restaurant and his position at ONCE; even our AI heroes have their limits! So he decided to sell the restaurant and again focus entirely on ONCE—where he has transformed the IT organization into the AI center for the company.

As CIO Cristian now leads an initiative called ONCE Innova, which brings together the business units (which at ONCE align with disability challenges, such as urban environments, home, rehabilitation, and training) and IT. The model he has put in place follows many of the principles and concepts you have read about in this book. The only difference is that instead of just focusing on improving business processes, at ONCE they also focus on improving the quality of life for their employees as well as the rest of the community with disabilities—they are not only removing barriers with technology, but using technology to remove barriers with life.

Cristian's team encourages new ideas from the business units and from ONCE affiliates by running idea contests in a growth-hacking mindset. They still collaborate closely with Microsoft and pioneered the use of Microsoft Seeing AI (*https://oreil.ly/AIO_7a-3*), an app that narrates the environment around you: it can describe the scene you are looking at, identify the people close to you, read restaurant menus and other documents, recognize paper currency to pay at a store, and more. Cristian himself can testify to the impact this app had on his life, not only in facilitating basic tasks but also allowing him to finally catch the jokes from his friends on WhatsApp who were sharing memes in their group all the time.

In city environments, ONCE is also unlocking the possibilities of smart cities applied to disabilities. With ambient AI, the city can describe itself, making people with disabilities aware of permanent barriers or temporary constructions. Ambient AI can also provide guidance to a destination, acting as a virtual guide dog or a virtual cane.

In this area ONCE has again collaborated with Microsoft on a promising technology called Soundscape (*https://oreil.ly/AIO_7a-4*) that uses 3D audio to provide a rich awareness of the user's surroundings, using audio cues as guidance. ONCE is bringing this technology to the Way of Saint James (or "Camino de Santiago"), a pilgrimage route followed each year by hundreds of thousands of pilgrims from more than 100 countries around the world in what is considered a spiritual retreat from modern life. Thanks to Soundscape, blind people will also be able to experience this life-changing journey: equipped with headphones, pilgrims will be guided with 3D audio cues along the path, providing the equivalent of an audio-based augmented reality experience.

I'm rooting for Cristian. I can't wait to see what else he will accomplish in his life, and the impact he will have on the lives of others. I do know this is just the beginning for him—not because he's a great leader and a brilliant mind (though he is), but because of his ability to reinvent himself.

Every time you think your company or your team is not prepared to embrace AI, that there's not enough talent or that the skills gap is too big, just think about Cristian. Maybe that gap is exactly what's needed to reenergize people and motivate them to achieve new accomplishments. Upskilling an organization can be a great opportunity to find new interests to pursue and new sources of joy, just like Cristian did when relearning to read or cook a grilled cheese sandwich. That approach is critical to building an AI organization, as you'll see in the next chapter when we discuss the *culture of talent*.

## 7

The Culture of Talent: Upskilling Your Organization

AI is a technology wave unlike any other we have experienced in the enterprise. The techniques used are radically different from the ones used in traditional software development. The business implications are also more profound than with any other wave we have seen in the past, with the potential to transform entire industries and completely redefine the processes in an organization. Many speak of AI as a fourth industrial revolution.

Such a big change in technology and business requires entirely new skills that, for the most part, organizations don't currently have. When asked by Gartner Research (*https://oreil.ly/AIO_7-1*) about the top blockers with regard to artificial intelligence for their organizations, CIOs identified "Lack of necessary staff skills" as the most important barrier, at a considerable distance from the next.

To contribute to the perfect storm, the AI revolution has happened so fast that new generations are not flooding out the gates of schools and training institutions—technical or business—with the required skills. This is leading to a skills shortage in the market that is severely impacting organizations.

The best way to address this crisis is by developing a *reskilling strategy*. This strategy should have a broad scope—the AI transformation will not be constrained to just some roles in your organization. Indeed, if you want to truly make the transition to an AI organization, every single function and level should be part of it.

A good way to structure the scope of this reskilling is according to the strategic model we have been using in this book, as shown in Figure 7-1.

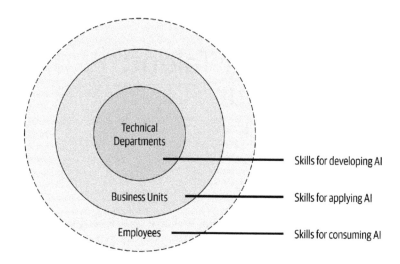

Figure 7-1. Skilling strategy for an AI organization

As you design your reskilling strategy, you will need to address three different major areas:

- Skills for technical departments so that they can provide the necessary supporting functions to the rest of the organization, as well as handling the development itself for those products with an in-house approach
- Skills for business units, which will play a fundamental role in applying AI to transform the business processes
- Skills for all employees, who can consume AI at different levels to support their decisions and optimize the way they work

Skills for Technical Departments

Technical departments are definitely the most affected by AI upskilling. Creating AI solutions requires a very different skill set than creating traditional software applications. However, AI is not always about building complex artificial neural network architectures. Technology vendors like Microsoft, Google Cloud, and Amazon Web Services provide lower-friction building blocks that don't require a deep knowledge of the most complex AI techniques. Existing software developers can easily learn these building blocks to modernize their applications and create new ones, like conversational agents. When building a reskilling program, you should start there. For example, the AI School (*https://oreil.ly/AIO_7-2*) provides a learning path focused on using prebuilt AI services, and another one focused on building conversational agents, neither of them requiring deep learning knowledge.

However, you shouldn't stop there. At some point you will need to create custom AI models that will require the technical departments to have those skills. At the very minimum, your organization will need personnel skilled in traditional machine learning, which uses algorithms that are well known and understood. These algorithms work on top of data, so accessing and preparing that data is also a required skill for this function. Data scientists already have that skill, so expanding to machine learning is usually a very natural path for them. That said, software developers can also develop this skill, and there are tools that can make it easier for them, such as autoML tools and high-level libraries like ML.NET (*https://oreil.ly/AIO_7-3*).

Finally, for the most complex scenarios, your organization will require deep learning skills. Deep learning may sound daunting, but there's already plenty of training content in programs such as the AI School to get started with the most typical artificial neural network architectures. Creating a state-of-the-art neural network from scratch requires significant skills and a continuous connection with the work done in the research community, but for the majority of organizations a good understanding of core deep learning concepts is enough to deliver outstanding results.

No matter what scope you want your technical departments to have—from consuming prebuilt AI services to creating sophisticated deep learning algorithms—you will always need them to have the required skills for the supporting functions that will be provided in-house. Even with a pure buy or outsource strategy, it's advisable that the technical teams deliver these functions, so they should be part of the skilling scope:

Architecture
> Although it doesn't require coding skills, defining an architecture for an AI solution requires a deep knowledge of the main technologies and techniques involved in big data and AI.

Infrastructure

> The infrastructure used in AI is significantly different from that in other workloads and involves managing highly distributed training farms on hardware such as GPUs or FPGAs, usually in the cloud. A good understanding of the computing associated with high-scale training and inference is a must in any AI team.

DevOps

> MLOps requires specialized skills to support the needs of the development teams, such as collaboration, continuous delivery, and traceability.

If you are aiming to develop new technologies to support your AI innovation, the supporting functions also include research. AI-applied research is an especially tricky area for resourcing because it is in extreme demand. The skills usually come from people with extensive background in machine learning, deep learning, and math, typically found in doctorates. For this reason, forming partnerships with universities or research institutions is a common approach in this case instead of building the skills in-house.

Skills for Business Units

When you're transforming your business processes, there will need to be symbiosis between your technical departments and your business units. The resulting multidisciplinary teams will have the critical role of defining the strategy for the business transformation, including the identification and prioritization of use cases for AI.

For this reason, business units should also be reskilled to be able to participate in this process. Otherwise, the gap between the business units and technology teams would be too wide for a meaningful dialogue between them.

At the very least, the individuals participating in this collaboration with the technical teams should be trained. These are usually "AI champions" in the business units or members of the management team. Ideally, the reskilling would be extended to all managers or individual contributors leading specific areas of the business. Training this entire community will make them more proactive about identifying opportunities and challenges to be solved with AI.

The extent of the skills required in the business units is not as deep as for technical teams. Business leaders don't need to learn *how* to develop AI, but instead *what* you can do with it. Typical areas to cover are:

- An overview of the core capabilities that AI can provide today. You can use the framework we used in the first chapter of this book: learning, perception, and cognition.

- Exploring the typical use cases AI can be applied to. Again, you can use the framework (and even the examples) that you have seen in this book: bring AI to every application, every business process, and every employee.

- Understanding the core processes involved in the AI transformation in an organization, including the key concepts explored in this book, such as team collaboration, data estate strategies, and ethics.

At Microsoft, we followed this approach for our finance organization. A first attempt to drive an AI transformation failed because it didn't involve the domain experts. In the second attempt, the entire organization was trained on the possibilities of AI and encouraged to propose the scenarios that might be most impactful for them. This led to the identification of forecasting as a top pain point for employees, who were involved in the entire development of the AI solution, and ended in the success story described in Chapter 3.

Skills for Any Employee

You have seen already in this book that the ultimate realization of the AI organization is to empower every employee with AI. For that to happen, every employee should also be part of your reskilling strategy. The level of skills depth required will depend on the scope that AI will have for the employee's function. We talked about three different requirements for empowering employees to participate in the AI transformation in Chapter 4, and the stage you're in will determine the skills required:

Democratization of knowledge
> With a data-first culture, you will hopefully have a consolidated data estate that includes easy-to-consume, highly semantic data accessible to every employee. Employees will need the skills to consume that knowledge and apply it to their tasks. For frontline workers, this could be as simple as making it accessible as part of their existing applications or through new conversational agents. For back office workers, it could also include more complex scenarios with advanced operations on top of that knowledge to

support their decision making, for example as part of their productivity applications like Office or business intelligence applications like PowerBI.

Democratization of AI consumption
When you add the ability for employees to apply AI on top of that knowledge, you will need them to have the basic skills to understand the concepts behind AI, as well as the AI models they will have available to them in the organization and the techniques to apply them to their own data.

Democratization of AI creation
Even the less complex techniques for AI creation, like automated machine learning and transfer learning, require a basic understanding of AI. This could be the same introduction to the core concepts required for business units, combined with a deeper exploration of the tools and techniques the employees will use to create their own AI.

Strategies for Talent Development

Now that you have an idea of the skills required for your technical departments, business units, and employees, the next step is usually an assessment of the current skills. The goal of this assessment is not to evaluate each employee's skills, but to understand the gaps across functions and business areas. The results of this assessment will guide your strategy for reskilling and help you design the AI training in your organization.

TECHNICAL TRAINING

Companies generally address technical training first. Many of the existing roles in any enterprise will map with the technical functions required but lack the incremental skills for AI, so training customized for each of these roles is highly recommended:

- Software developers have the core skills required for using prebuilt AI services and creating conversational agents. They are also great candidates for embracing custom AI development with machine learning.

- Data scientists are already very familiar with data preparation and statistical analysis, so machine learning and even deep learning are natural extensions for them.

- Data engineers and distributed systems architects are excellent candidates to also manage the infrastructure required for AI.

- DevOps managers have a lot of experience with supporting software development teams throughout the product lifecycle, and software architects are already defining business requirements and architecture design for software solutions. Because of that, they both have strong potential to meet the MLOps and AI architecture needs of the organization.

There are many approaches to address the required upskilling for existing roles. For technical roles, options include onsite training offered by specialized consulting companies, online training (either paid or free) to be consumed on demand, or MOOCs (massive open online courses) delivered by online platforms such as Coursera, edX, or Udacity. Technology vendors also provide training options, such as the Microsoft AI School mentioned earlier, which is based on the same technical training we developed internally for our technical employees.

BUSINESS TRAINING

For business units—including leaders, managers, and business users—there are fewer training options, but many business schools are now offering master's programs, courses, and shorter sessions to help business leaders understand AI and how to embrace it. Some of those institutions also offer online equivalents, either paid or free. At Microsoft, we provide training for business leaders as well through the AI Business School (*https://oreil.ly/AIO_7-4*). The AI Business School is the big brother of this book; it has a similar structure with plenty of real use cases and examples to learn from other business leaders.

A common approach we see in many companies is to "Train the Trainers." The AI team, in whatever shape it has for the company, gets deeper into highly specialized training with any of the previously mentioned options. After that specialization, they act as a catalyzer for the training in other teams and departments. This approach has many advantages because they can deliver the training in a way that is uniquely adapted to the organization and its business context. It's not uncommon for that training to be scaled to the entire company, including back office and even frontline employees.

A variation of this concept is the *hackathon*. Hackathons are events that bring technical employees together to focus on one or many challenges or ideas. Their duration varies, usually from a day to a week, and it's not only an excellent approach to develop the organization's technical skills, but also a great way to foster new ideas coming directly from the employees. When opened to external participation, these hackathons are also great sources for hiring new talent. Microsoft's internal hackathon brings together every year around 20,000 employees spanning 400 cities and 75 countries, working on thousands of different projects ideated by the participants. Many of these projects emerge as future products or technologies in Microsoft, such as the eye control in Windows 10 and the adaptive controller for Xbox.

Hiring for the AI Organization

Most companies complement the upskilling of existing roles with a hiring strategy to bring new talent to the organization. The same principles apply to hiring —it is important to have a good balance of AI experience among both technically specialized roles and business management roles.

Not all the hires have to be AI researchers (although some wouldn't hurt!). The skills we have previously covered also apply for new hires, from roles closer to software development who can create intelligent applications and conversational agents, to roles closer to data science who can apply machine learning, to roles focused on supporting functions (such as MLOps, architecture, or infrastructure), to business and technical management roles.

When hiring, we can also look out for other skills to make sure the candidates are appropriate for the working style needed in an AI organization:

- They should be open to an agile environment. No matter what role you are hiring for, candidates should show signs that they can work in a very agile environment, continuously connected with the customers' needs, owning the end-to-end experience, and delivering products in an iterative fashion.

- They should be able to function in a highly collaborative environment, working very closely with other members in the team as a unit instead of just producing individual deliverables in a vacuum. They should also be comfortable with cross-group collaboration.

- They should be passionate about or at least somehow connected to the company's business. Even technical roles will work in close partnership with the business, and a good understanding of the industry will facilitate that communication.

- They should be representative of your customers' diversity. A common challenge in many organizations is the lack of diversity in their teams. In the next chapter you will learn how AI can present new challenges, such as bias and unfairness. A great way to minimize those challenges is to have a diverse team, who will naturally create products with diversity in mind. Diverse hiring is not only a social responsibility that companies have; it is requirement if they want their products to be relevant for as broad a cross-section of society as possible.

AI Hero: Cathy

My son Guillermo told me something some time ago that made me think. He said he wanted to learn computer programming, which probably made me the happiest parent on earth, but he asked for one condition: I had to be with him the entire time. My kids don't usually ask their parents for help with homework, so why was Guillermo suddenly asking for it? "I'm afraid I may create an AI that turns against me," was his answer.

Setting aside how little that says about me and my abilities to provide my own family with confidence in AI, Guillermo's comment was a symptom of something bigger. If society doesn't trust AI, how is it going to have any positive impact on it?

AI has huge potential to help solve society's most pressing challenges. Great people are making others' lives better by dedicating their own to research into new cures for diseases, inclusion of people with disabilities, environmental protection, refugee assistance, and natural disaster intervention, among many other examples.

Empowering those great people with AI can help humanity to take a new look at the problems we are facing. Every single aspect of our lives can potentially be augmented and improved with AI. The positive transformation that AI can create in society is just beginning, and new innovative applications are being introduced every day.

But for positive transformation to happen, AI has to be trusted by society. Every single technological disruption in history has required a careful balance between the development of technology and its safety. For example, many breakthroughs had to be made for aviation to be used safely at scale and enable the global impact it has today, and we had to learn how to transport electricity safely before it could power our cities and homes.

In the same way, we need to develop safe AI and balance its accelerated pace of development with protections against its potential risks. AI development is leading to challenging questions: What are the risks of AI to user privacy? How do we make sure AI algorithms don't learn unfair or biased behaviors from real-world biases? Who is accountable for the decisions made by AI?

These questions and many others require a different breed of hero. Previous transformations have required heroes focused on the technology. Aviation, electricity, and software made progress because of genius innovators who took the technology a little bit further in every iteration. AI is different. It connects with humans at a deeper level, and it has the potential to participate in impactful decisions affecting many areas of our lives as it proliferates in health care, financial services, transportation, and education. Therefore, it requires heroes who can combine technological innovation with a humanistic approach, analytical thinking with social skills, left brain with right brain.

Cathy (*https://oreil.ly/AIO_8a-1*) has worked at EY, a global leader in assurance, tax, transaction, and advisory services, for 26 years. She is a social innovator who comfortably moves between these opposing dynamisms every day. Her left brain–right brain balance is embedded in her DNA, and in conjunction with her innate curiosity for learning, it has motivated Cathy's balanced approach to AI.

Being from a small town in rural Saskatchewan (Canada) with limited scholastic resources didn't hold Cathy back from pursuing a life-long love of learning, just like bullying, blindness, poverty, or a family disease didn't stop the other AI heroes in this book. When her high school didn't offer physics, Cathy took it by correspondence and re-created lab experiments at home. With no local museums or even a movie theatre, Cathy leveraged her small public library to learn about the rest of the world through books.

Having a father who was an early adopter of technology gave Cathy access to computers at a very young age. It was while playing a video game for the Commodore 64 that another of Cathy's passions surfaced. In the classic Lemonade Stand game, players make decisions about different aspects of running a lemonade stand, like pricing, stock, and advertising, based on external factors like the weather and competitors. The uncertainty of the results and the delicate balance required to maximize growth while keeping risk low fascinated Cathy—so much so that she enrolled in the University of Waterloo's Masters of Accounting program, and joined EY as part of its co-op program.

Cathy's atypical combination of interests spanning technology, accounting, and social issues didn't take long to show up. In her time working at EY she has made use of her accounting background and CPA designation to navigate the balance between business and societal interests, not only with new technologies but also broader social issues including climate change, sustainability, social inclusion, and diversity. Throughout her career she has acted as a bridge between opposing interests, trying to find common ground.

From the mainframe to ERP systems to ecommerce, Cathy has experienced the evolution of technology firsthand and observed the growing trust challenges created by each new technological innovation. She managed the risks of the first distributed computers automating tasks that were previously performed by humans. She evaluated the sufficiency of mechanisms to ensure data protection and privacy as financial systems became web-enabled, and she had to think about how to avoid fraud, cyber-crime, and money laundering as digitization and compute power increased. In a nutshell, Cathy's role is to always ask, "What can go wrong?"

When AI started to sound like the next step in the technology journey, Cathy was already there. Driven by her personal interests, she was thinking about the potential risks of scaling AI at the enterprise level even before AI was in the enterprise. She started to share her opinions on the topic with EY colleagues, customers, LinkedIn followers, and even her book club. Cathy lives by EY's motto: "The better the question. The better the answer. The better the world works."— and AI had a lot of questions to be answered.

Based on this early interest in managing the risks of AI, Cathy was asked to take on the role of EY's Global Trusted AI Advisory Leader in 2018. Since then, she's had the huge challenge of setting the strategy at EY to help customers across the most regulated and mission-critical industries to responsibly embrace artificial intelligence.

To meet this challenge Cathy used a similar approach to the one you will learn about in the next chapter. Instead of starting with processes or technologies, she focused on identifying the outcome. What does responsible AI look like? What is needed for users to trust in AI?

To answer these questions, Cathy worked with a global team of individuals at EY with diverse backgrounds to define the unique attributes for their organization, aligned with the company's values—the first step in any responsible AI journey. After three months of close partnership between representatives from EY's Technology Risk, Data and Analytics, Innovation, Assurance, and IT

Advisory teams, the company released its list of trusted AI attributes: *performance, transparency, explainability, resiliency,* and *unbiased.* (We will look in detail at Microsoft's equivalent attributes, which are strongly aligned with these, in the next chapter.)

Cathy's contribution didn't end with the development of EY's trusted AI attributes, though; in fact, that was just the beginning. She quickly recognized the importance of fitting the ethical and social considerations for AI into the existing enterprise governance. Trust in AI can be achieved only if the trust attributes are embedded across the organization and throughout the AI development lifecycle.

EY already had such a lifecycle in place (MLOps, which you learned about in Chapter 5), but it needed to be redefined to make sure the trust attributes were enforced. The result was the launch of EY's Trusted AI Framework, which mapped the trust attributes to the AI development lifecycle. This framework includes a three-step process to promote trust in AI initiatives in the company:

Purposeful design
> Design and build systems that purposefully integrate the right balance of robotic, intelligent, and autonomous capabilities to advance well-defined business goals, mindful of context, constraints, readiness and risks.

Agile governance
> Track emergent issues across social, regulatory, reputational, and ethical domains to inform processes that govern the integrity of a system, its uses, architecture and embedded components, data sourcing and management, model training, and monitoring.

Vigilant supervision
> Continuously fine-tune, curate and monitor systems to ensure reliability in performance, identify and remediate bias, promote transparency and inclusiveness.

Changing the entire development lifecycle in an organization to take into account the AI trust principles is not an easy task. As Cathy went through this journey, she identified best practices that she now recommends to EY's customers. One of these is creating an AI advisory board that can work with the organization to determine which use cases to apply AI to and bring in broader ethical and social considerations. It's important for the AI advisory board to ask not only "Can we use AI?" but also "Should we?"

Other practices recommended by EY include awareness training for executives and developers, as well as design standards for the development of AI that incorporate a detailed risk and control framework. We'll discuss these and other governance practices in more detail in the next chapter.

Cathy compares these practices to the way she taught her twin daughters how to ride a bike: it took patience and the appropriate safeguards, in the form of training wheels, parental supervision, and a controlled environment, to avoid early falls. And even after they'd learned the basics it was important to stay vigilant, as her daughters could still suffer a mishap as they moved into new terrain, rode faster, or tried new things like going hands-free. AI is very similar. It should be trained and operated with appropriate safeguards that match its capabilities and limitations, and continuous monitoring mechanisms need to be put in place to provide early warning if it fails or begins to show suboptimal performance in new terrains or capabilities.

Cathy's twin daughters, like any other children, will always push to test their limits. Companies will similarly want to push the limits of how they can utilize new technologies like AI. Your role in both cases is to make sure that happens in a safe environment, understanding the limitations at each step and putting the appropriate safeguards in place. As a business or technical leader, you will play a big role in the sustainable development of AI in your company. Establishing a strong culture of responsibility in your organization will be critical to develop AI that can be trusted by your employees and your customers, and ultimately to contribute to the societal impact of AI.

I won't cover how to ride a bike in this book, but in the next chapter you do learn how to set up the AI training wheels for your company. First, I will cover some key principles you should consider for AI development. Then, you will learn key practices to put those principles to work in your governance processes.

## 8

The Culture of Ethics: Responsible AI

As a business or technical leader, you will play a big role in the sustainable development of AI. Putting in place a strong culture of responsibility in your organization will be critical to developing AI that can be trusted by your employees and your customers, and ultimately to contributing to the overall future impact of AI in society.

The first step in this journey is to understand and acknowledge the challenges associated with AI, and define the principles that will guide how your company will address those challenges.

Responsible AI Principles

We went through this same journey at Microsoft, which led us to define the six principles (*https://oreil.ly/AIO_8-1*) that we believe should guide the development of AI: fairness, reliability and safety, privacy and security, inclusiveness, transparency, and accountability. We defined those principles very early in our AI transformation journey, which has allowed us to learn valuable insights into the process and develop technology that we also offer to our customers to help them design and operate AI responsibly. Let's examine those six principles in more detail.

FAIRNESS

AI is designed by humans and trained on data coming from the real world, and unfortunately the real world can be unfair and biased. If an AI model for a loan assessment is trained on historical data where credit agents were biased in their decisions, the AI model will also carry that bias. If another AI model that identifies sales opportunities is based on past opportunities from a sales department that favored leads with some unconscious bias, the AI model will do the same.

Even if the training data hasn't been influenced by human bias, it may not be representative enough of certain groups, causing the AI model to not work properly for those groups. For example, a medical AI model trained only on Caucasians' features may not work correctly for other races, and a facial recognition algorithm may not work correctly for ethnicities not well represented in the training set.

And the issue may be even subtler. AI models may be based on datasets that do represent the current world accurately, but help perpetuate inequalities or types of unfair treatment that are already present in the world. For example, when my sister, an architect, visits a construction site with her male business partner, construction workers naturally look at him when asking questions. My manager, Mitra Azizirad, is a corporate vice president at Microsoft. She joined Microsoft as an engineer for the US Department of Defense, became the first female Chief Technology Officer, and then moved into leading the public sector business. Still, when I have lunch with her it's not rare for waiters to hand the bill to me, a guy who was playing with his Commodore 64 while Mitra was meeting with four-star generals about critical government issues. As humans, we make those mistakes because we unconsciously make assumptions based on clichés, past experiences, and ingrained societal expectations.

AI models will make the same mistakes if not designed properly. Natural language processing is a good example of this. These models are based on word embedding techniques, which can exhibit sexist behavior even if trained on what we might think of as gender-neutral sources such as news articles. Words like "receptionist" and "nurse" are closer to "female" than they are to "male" in the vector space. Others, like "computer programmer" and "boss," are closer to "male" than they are to "female." Any AI system built on top of this representation will inherit that bias—for example, a translation model could translate the gender-neutral Spanish sentence "Es recepcionista" to a gender-specific sentence in English, assuming it was referring to a woman ("She is a receptionist").

Avoiding bias

How can we address these issues? Although there are techniques and technologies that can help with detecting and avoiding bias, it is the people designing and operating these algorithms who should ultimately be conscious of the potential consequences of bias in AI.

Therefore, first off, it's important to include people with relevant subject matter expertise in the design process. Domain experts will be best equipped to detect and understand the subtleties of dataset bias, underrepresentation, and unintended associations. Credit experts should be part of the design process for a credit scoring AI system, sellers should contribute to an opportunity prioritization model, and doctors should be involved in designing medical AI models.

It can also be helpful to use techniques like *datasheets for datasets* (*https:// oreil.ly/AIO_8-2*). Just as the US government requires food manufacturers to document the ingredients on food packages, datasheets for datasets proposes a standard approach to document the inputs for AI systems, making biases easier to spot before they affect people. Datasheets provide an opportunity for domain experts to communicate what they know about a dataset and its limitations to the developers who might use it. This way, a developer can understand how the data is meant to be used and the potential ethical considerations when applying it to an AI model.

There are also many ongoing efforts to use analytical techniques to detect and address potential unfairness, like methods that systematically assess the data used to train AI models for appropriate representativeness and unintended associations. For example, IBM Research has released AI Fairness 360 (*https:// oreil.ly/AIO_8-3*), a toolkit of metrics to check for unwanted bias in datasets and models.

Other techniques can also help to fix that bias automatically. For example, at Microsoft, our researchers are working on techniques to identify bias in word embeddings (*https://oreil.ly/AIO_8-4*) and correct it, enabling natural language processing scenarios built on top of these models to be fair. Gender bias can be removed by modifying the representations of words with biased associations ("receptionist," "boss," "software developer") to be equally associated with men and women.

Additionally, if the recommendations or predictions made by the AI system can have important consequences for people (economical, physical, emotional, or any other), it is critical that the domain experts are also part of the decision loop. These experts should be trained to understand the limitations of the system, recognizing situations in which people can make decisions more holistically and empathetically and making sure technical systems are not viewed as more authoritative than humans.

When humans and machines work together in this way, the overall accuracy achieved is much higher than either of them can attain separately. The system combines the best qualities of each, and there is full accountability for the decisions made.

Kriti, our AI hero who used AI to help abuse victims in South Africa and girls in India, has experienced the gender bias rooted in society firsthand, not only in her childhood but in her professional life.

Kriti is a big fan of open source and has made the code for her projects available on GitHub so that people in other countries can use, customize, extend, and contribute to them—effectively enabling her work to scale globally. She also regularly participates in online open source forums and contributes code to various projects.

However, a while ago Kriti noticed that she was getting questioned about her technical abilities more than one might expect for someone with her level of experience. When she was participating in conversations in communities like Slack, people would often ask about her background and skills. Code she contributed to other open source projects would also get a lot of scrutiny.

So Kriti did an experiment. She changed her username in those channels to a male-specific name and replaced her profile picture with a picture of a cat with a jet pack. The change she observed in her interactions with other members of these communities was significant: people were much less likely to question her qualifications or the quality of her code.

The technology world has fallen into a dangerous cycle in which the contributions of women are less valued, and therefore women are less interested in technical roles, perpetuating their underrepresentation. If the people developing AI are not diverse, how can the technologies they create be?

RELIABILITY AND SAFETY

AI has an amazing potential to improve people's safety. It can assist us in performing activities such as driving or operating machinery, greatly increasing their safety. It can even replace us in hazardous situations, such as when we need to work with toxic materials or conduct inspections in unsafe environments.

However, as we leverage AI for more and more critical scenarios, reliability will have to be assured. Like any emerging technology, AI needs to follow a maturity cycle and we should not go beyond its limitations at any stage, putting in place the right safeguards.

Testing and monitoring

These safeguards start with rigorous testing. AI systems should be able to operate as they were originally designed to, respond to unanticipated conditions, and resist harmful manipulation. Rigorous testing involves a carefully planned staged implementation process, so the system can be thoroughly tested before a large-scale implementation. Simulation technologies can help us train and test AI systems in the complete safety of a virtual environment. For example, Microsoft's AirSim (*https://oreil.ly/AIO_8-5*) is a high-fidelity system that provides realistic environments for training and testing autonomous systems such as robots, drones, or cars to be sure they can operate safely before they are tested in the real world.

After testing, it is equally important that organizations properly maintain and monitor their AI systems. Contrary to traditional software development, AI always operates using probabilistic approaches. This means that we should always be aware of their accuracy and make sure this accuracy is within acceptable limits for reliability and safety. AI systems degrade over time due to changing factors in the environment that were not reflected in the training data. To address this issue, using a telemetry system to provide real-time accuracy reporting for your AI models, as well as a dashboard and notification system across all the AI systems, is critical. As discussed in Chapter 5, an AI organization should have an agile MLOps cycle that can quickly detect the degradation of any system and be able to fix it even faster, tracing the root cause back to the original assets behind that system (such as the code and datasets used), and should be able to deploy the corrected system continuously.

It's important to involve domain experts throughout this process, because they can help spot when the performance of an AI system is degrading as well as identifying other problems, such as bias. As part of our monitoring strategy, we should evaluate when and how an AI system should seek human input during any of the critical situations that might arise, and how it should transfer control to a human if needed.

PRIVACY AND SECURITY

To create AI solutions that are relevant to users, the underlying data must also be relevant to them—which of course makes privacy and security even more important than ever. Users' confidence in sharing relevant data has to be earned, and that can be achieved only when their privacy is protected and secured. AI, like any other technology, should also comply with privacy laws that require transparency about the collection, use, and storage of data.

Data collection, use, and storage

The amazing scenarios enabled by AI may tempt an organization's employees to collect new data from its customers. Without proper centralization and management, that could result in a lack of control over the collection of data across teams, and privacy risks that are difficult to detect.

After the data is collected, the use of that data has to be managed as well. The collected data should include relevant information such as the terms governing its collection, and processes must be put in place to control and audit the access and use of the data in any AI system to ensure that it complies with those terms.

Finally, data should be stored in a way that prevents bad actors from gaining access to private information or inflicting harm. Technology can be very effective at protecting data. For example, cryptography techniques like homomorphic encryption (*https://oreil.ly/AIO_8-6*) can enable us to store the sensitive data encrypted in our systems and still apply AI models to it. Azure confidential computing (*https://oreil.ly/AIO_8-7*) provides Trusted Execution Environments (TEEs) that protect the data they use from being accessed outside of them, which makes them ideal for multiple organizations to use to train AI models without physically sharing the data among them.

Responding to security threats

AI also brings new threats and types of attacks. Organizations must be prepared to adequately respond to these evolving privacy and security threats. We were reminded of these new threats at Microsoft when we released a bot on Twitter called Tay, following the success of the equivalent social bot in China, Xiaoice. Tay learned from online interactions with users to better replicate human communication and personality traits. However, within 24 hours a coordinated attack began to feed Tay with bigoted rhetoric, turning it from a polite bot to a vehicle for hate speech. We of course had to shut down the bot immediately, delete the offending messages, and issue an apology taking full responsibility. This unfortunate episode taught us an important lesson about the vulnerability of AI to attacks that influence training datasets, especially for systems with automatic learning capabilities. To help mitigate this threat in the future, the team developed technologies such as advanced content filters and introduced supervisors for AI systems that have automatic learning capabilities. The lessons learned from Tay and many other AI-based security experiences were also compiled into a paper (*https://oreil.ly/AIO_8-8*) to help other enterprises better prepare their AI systems for these new privacy and security threats.

INCLUSIVENESS

AI will redefine how companies and governments interact with customers and citizens. Just like the internet 20 years ago, AI will open up new channels for that interaction to happen, creating a new world of possibilities.

But like with the internet, those creating these new channels will have the big responsibility of making them accessible to the broadest possible user base. Enterprises should adopt inclusive design practices to help developers and designers understand the importance of inclusiveness and learn techniques to make their AI systems widely accessible, without unintentionally excluding certain segments of the population.

Accessibility and inclusive design

Accessibility standards and regulations should of course be part of this process. The European Accessibility Act (*https://oreil.ly/AIO_8-9*) will regulate common accessibility requirements covering a broad range of products and services such as computer devices, websites, ATMs, and media. It is not as well known as its equivalent for privacy, the General Data Protection Regulation (GDPR) (*https://oreil.ly/AIO_8-10*), but it will also enable positive changes in the way companies create their products and services for accessibility. Other legislation is already in place in other geographies, like the Communications and Video Accessibility Act (*https://oreil.ly/AIO_8-11*) in the US and the UN Convention on the Rights of Persons with Disabilities (*https://oreil.ly/AIO_8-12*), which has been ratified by 160 countries.

However, inclusiveness is about much more than complying with accessibility standards. Ideally, accessibility and inclusive design work together to make experiences that are not only compliant with standards, but truly open to and usable by all. In 2001, the World Health Organization evolved the definition of disability (*https://oreil.ly/AIO_8-13*) to expand it beyond the classical notion of a personal health condition to a broader, context-dependent one. Think about being in a foreign country where you don't speak the local language, or replying to an email while driving, or using a touch interface with gloves. AI systems should be accessible in all the contexts they will be used in.

That definition takes a comprehensive approach we call *inclusive design* (*https://oreil.ly/AIO_8-14*). Inclusive design is a methodology that enables and draws on the full range of human diversity. It is not about making one thing for all people, but instead about designing diverse ways for everyone to participate in an experience with a sense of belonging. It is anchored in three principles:

Recognize exclusion
Think of points of exclusion as just mismatched experiences that can apply to any individual, instead of focusing on personal health conditions.

Learn from diversity
Create empathy by spending time understanding the experience from diverse real perspectives.

Solve for one, extend to many
Design with hard constraints, but expand to work across a spectrum of related abilities. For example, designing for the hard of hearing community can benefit people using their second language or in a crowded airport.

On top of these universal design methodologies for human–computer interactions, AI also brings unique challenges. AI-infused systems can contradict well-established usability guidelines for traditional user interface design. For example, the principles of consistency and predictability are often not followed by systems powered by AI, which always bring some level of uncertainty.

At Microsoft, this was an area of research that culminated in the publication of the "Guidelines for Human–AI Interaction" (*https://oreil.ly/AIO_8-15*), a complete set of 18 design guidelines that cover aspects such as the initial context that should be provided by the system, how to manage interactions, how to react when something goes wrong, and how to behave over time.

Using these and other guidelines, you should be able to create AI systems that can be used by the entire diversity of humans. However, AI can go beyond that. Not only do we have the responsibility to create AI systems that are accessible, but we can also use AI to remove existing barriers, bringing people forward.

There are one billion people in the world with some kind of disability, who often struggle to get equal access to the opportunities that the other 6.5 billion people have. AI, unlike some of the preceding technological revolutions, has the ability to reduce this gap and actually remove existing obstacles for these people instead of adding to them. AI can create entirely new ways of interaction that reduce barriers in areas such as employment, education, and even overall quality of life.

Rochester Institute of Technology (RIT) uses the Presentation Translator (*https://oreil.ly/AIO_8-16*) in PowerPoint to generate real-time speech-to-text captions during lectures and discussions in its classrooms. This helps students who are deaf or hard of hearing to get the same information at the same time as their hearing peers—something that was previously not possible, without AI. Speakers of English as a second language can also benefit from this feature, as they can use an app on their laptops or mobile devices to get real-time captions in the language of their choice.

I've already mentioned another great example of how AI can remove barriers between people and their environment: Helpicto, an application developed by the French company Equadex that helps children with autism spectrum disorder to communicate with others. In AI hero Cristian's story, you also heard about Microsoft Seeing AI and Microsoft Soundscape, which are apps that help people with limited vision to understand and navigate the world around them. These are just a few examples of ways that AI can be used to break down barriers and promote accessibility and inclusiveness.

TRANSPARENCY

Transparency is a core principle that helps support the five others we're discussing here. Without transparency, how can we identify any bias causing unfairness? How can we check whether a model's output is based on premises that are wrong?

In traditional software development, explaining why the program ended with a particular result is relatively simple: programs follow concrete steps, and we can easily walk back the steps to debug how a certain outcome was obtained. In AI systems, it's not so simple. Rules are inferred based on the data used for training. In some cases, like in modern AI techniques such as deep learning, the inferred rules are not even legible. Modern algorithms act as "black boxes," with no visibility of what is happening inside.

A dangerous pattern for AI development is when developers or data scientists create these opaque models, disconnecting domain experts from their inner workings. It is important that people with subject matter expertise can understand the decisions made by an AI system and ultimately confirm that the system is reliable.

The importance of domain knowledge

Abraham Wald (*https://oreil.ly/AIO_8-17*) was a Hungarian mathematician who worked for the Statistical Research Group in Manhattan during World War II, where he applied statistics to various wartime problems. One of the problems was to decide where to provide additional fuselage protection to minimize bomber losses to enemy fire. Armor helped diminish the effects of a hit, but it also made the plane heavier and more difficult to maneuver.

The team had access to the historical data from the American bombers coming back from engagements in Europe: the locations of bullet holes were recorded, offering an interesting view of their distribution across the fuselage (see Figure 8-1).

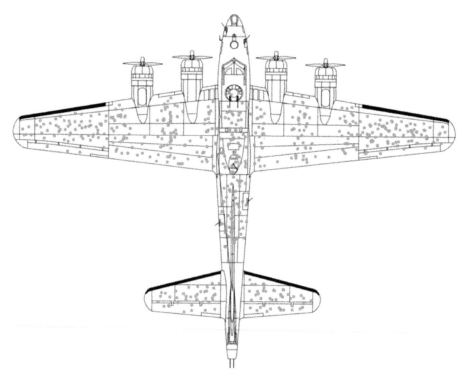

Figure 8-1. Bullet impacts on WWII bombers

Without domain expertise, any mathematician in the Statistical Research Group looking at images like these would likely have recommended reinforcing the wings, tailplanes, and core body of all the bombers. Abraham Wald instructed the military to do the exact opposite, recommending that the areas less impacted by bullets, like the engines and the cockpit, be reinforced with armor. The reason was simple: if those areas didn't have many impacts it wasn't because they were rarely hit, it was simply because the planes that got hit in those places weren't coming back.

An AI model would never recognize that subtlety, which is why people with domain knowledge have to be involved in the design and debugging of AI systems, and why those systems must be understandable to them.

Let's consider another example that we worked on at Microsoft. In the mid-1990s, Cost-Effective Healthcare (CEHC) funded a large multi-institutional project (*https://oreil.ly/AIO_8-18*) to evaluate the use of a machine learning model to predict the risk for patients with pneumonia admitted to the hospital. The model learned that patients with asthma were at lower risk than the general population, and therefore recommended that those patients not be hospitalized. But any doctor would know it is actually the opposite: patients with asthma are actually at much higher risk if they get pneumonia and therefore should be prioritized in the hospital admissions.

What could have led to this result? Because all doctors know about this elevated risk, the dataset was biased. Any asthmatic patient admitted with pneumonia went directly to the intensive care unit, lowering the risk for those patients dramatically. As this example shows, if the data scientists creating the model are not aware of such factors, they can easily create a black-box model in which these unintended effects are not detected.

Microsoft Research has been working on these issues for many years. One of the techniques it developed is called GA2M (*https://oreil.ly/AIO_8-19*), for Generalized Additive Models + interactions. With this technique, we can understand the decisions made by the model, and involve domain experts to validate the behavior. In the pneumonia example, doctors would be involved in the decision-making process and would be able to use their understanding of the factors involved to validate the choices made.

As AI becomes more pervasive in our lives, transparency is not going to be just a matter of reliability—it is going to be a user requirement. Users are asking more and more for the reasons behind the decisions made or influenced by AI models: Why am I seeing this ad? Why was my loan application denied? Why is my customer going to churn, and what can I do to avoid it? To answer those kinds of questions companies will need to implement fully traceable processes as part of their MLOps cycle, like the ones you learned about in Chapter 5. All the assets used to create the AI system have to be traceable to the particular user instance, and the model itself will need to be explainable so that we can better understand each decision made and describe the reason to the user in simple terms: you are seeing this ad because you visited these two websites in the past; your loan was denied because of the size of your mortgage compared with your salary; and your customer will churn because of an unusual number of support incidents with negative feedback.

ACCOUNTABILITY

In a sense, the previous five principles lead into this one. Who is ultimately responsible for an AI system working reliably? Who should be held accountable for an unfair decision made on the basis of an AI recommendation? Who's on point to guarantee user privacy, or to assure nobody is excluded?

As AI systems become more and more autonomous, there's a general fear that the answer to all these questions is *nobody*. That is not acceptable. The people who design, deploy, and operate an AI system should also be accountable for how the system works, as well as the decisions affected by it. As with any other technology or product, we should establish accountability norms in our organizations that ultimately make us responsible for all of these things.

The only difference for AI compared with other technologies is where the boundaries for accountability may lie. For highly automated AI systems, the accountability for the creator should be higher. Autonomous vehicle manufacturers will certainly have a higher scope of responsibility than traditional ones, because some decisions previously relying on the driver are now dependent on the design of the system. As we develop AI in our organizations, we should be aware of these responsibilities and establish the right accountability chain to make sure it's well understood by all of the teams involved.

For AI systems that are not automating decisions but supporting them, the issue of accountability is much trickier. Even if we could argue that the final responsibility lies with the individual or company operating the system, the operator's expectations could be different. In those cases, clear communication is absolutely critical. We need to make sure the system positions the recommendation with the right expectations; for example, highlighting the error rate, limitations, and context for it. We should also be transparent about the main factors affecting the decision, for instance using the traceability techniques outlined in the previous section. But even if we're clear about the limitations of the system and we explain its decisions, humans can easily fall into the trap of the "automation addiction," which makes us lower our attention or lose our skills when we are being supported by automated systems.

And this brings us to a third important aspect of accountability—monitoring. Continuous monitoring and maintenance of an AI system is central to accountability. For creators, this means being prescriptive about the maintenance processes needed, as well as assuring that the operators of the system are trained and equipped to maintain it. Systems can become inaccurate beyond an admissible threshold over time because of changes in the environment or the data. People using those systems may become so used to them that they don't apply their own judgment anymore, also impacting the final accuracy. A doctor with a 95% diagnosis accuracy rate could improve that to 99% by complementing their decisions with an AI system with a 90% accuracy rate. But if the doctor relied entirely on the system, the overall accuracy would drop to that 90%.

The Responsible AI Development Lifecycle

On July 13, 2001, webmasters all over the world started to see a weird request in their web server logs:

```
GET /default.ida?NNNNNNNNNNNNNNNNNNNNNNNNNNNNNNNNNNNNNNNNNNNNNNNNNNNNN
NNNNNNNNNNNNNNNNNNNNNNNNNNNNNNNNNNNNNNNNNNNNNNNNNNNNNNNNNNNNNNNNNNNNNNN
NNNNNNNNNNNNNNNNNNNNNNNNNNNNNNNNNNNNNNNNNNNNNNNNNNNNNNNNNNNNNNNNNNNNNNN
NNNNNNNNNNNNNNNNNNNNNNNNNNNNNNNNNN%u9090%u6858%ucbd3%u7801%u9090%u6858
%ucbd3%u7801%u9090%u6858%ucbd3%u7801%u9090%u9090%u8190%u00c3%u0003%u8
b00%u531b%u53ff%u0078%u0000%u00=a
```

The request used a technique known as *buffer overflow*. The concept is simple: when an application takes an input from the user (for example, a piece of text), the result is copied into memory. If the developer is not careful and doesn't truncate the input, it can overflow the space the developer saved for it, overwriting memory that was intended for something different. With some skill, you can design an input that turns into computer instructions which are then executed on the targeted computer without the user's knowledge or consent.

This particular request used a bug in the Microsoft web server at the time (Internet Information Services, or IIS). It filled the entire buffer reserved for the input with the letter *N*, and followed this with a set of codified malicious instructions that would execute on the server.

In this case the instructions did three things, all really bad:

- Overrode the response for all the site's pages with a message stating the website had been hacked, bringing web servers around the world offline

- Sent web requests to particular blocks of IP addresses, including one belonging to the White House's web servers, causing them to collapse

- Sent the same attacking request to more web servers, multiplying itself

By July 19 more than 300,000 servers had been infected by the worm, at a peak rate of 2,000 per minute. Fortunately, the worm (known as Code Red) was programmed to stop propagating on July 20 and wait until the beginning of the following month to continue spreading. In a crazy race against the clock, webmasters all over the world had to scramble to patch their systems before August 1 to avoid the collapse of the internet.

Just when we thought Code Red was under control, an even more devastating worm called Nimda (the reverse spelling of Admin) was released on September 18, this time targeting not only web servers but any workstation connected to the internet using Windows—which at that time was almost every computer on the planet. Nimda was much more sophisticated than Code Red; it used multiple infection methods and would also infect files. Because of that, it quickly spread to affect half of the companies in the world, with many of them needing to fully disconnect their servers from the internet to do the necessary repairs. The economic damage had no precedent in the industry.

Microsoft was at the center of the controversy. This evidence of the devastating potential impact of security vulnerabilities exploited by attackers was a huge wake-up call for the company. In January 2002, Bill Gates sent an internal memo announcing the Trustworthy Computing initiative (*https://oreil.ly/AIO_8-20*). It acknowledged the problem and laid out a set of principles for the company to strive for (availability, security, and privacy). However, solving the challenges of the new era of computing required a completely new way of creating software. The Security Development Lifecycle (*https://oreil.ly/AIO_8-21*) was created as a mandatory policy for all Microsoft teams and published externally for everyone to use. It introduced security and privacy throughout all phases of the development process, and despite some initial skepticism, it is broadly identified as having had a huge influence on making today's computer systems more secure (*https://oreil.ly/AIO_8-22*).

Responsible AI development has many similarities with Trustworthy Computing. It also requires more than a set of principles or a company-wide communication; it requires changing the way AI is developed. Just as Trustworthy Computing required the Security Development Lifecycle, responsible AI will require a responsible AI development lifecycle.

The good news is that you should already have defined an AI development lifecycle. In Chapter 5, you learned how AI requires a comprehensive approach in the organization, from design to production, called MLOps. MLOps is not only helpful for managing the quality and impact of your AI development, it also provides a hugely convenient mechanism to enforce a governance process for responsible AI.

If you want your AI principles to be more than just words on paper, you should translate them into clear activities, guidelines, and validation processes that are infused throughout your entire MLOps process. As you'll recall, that process was the combination of three different loops: definition, development, and operations.

DEFINITION

Responsible AI development should be considered as early as the definition stages. In many instances, projects are misaligned with the company's principles from their inception. Maybe the use case itself compromises your responsible approach. Maybe it doesn't, but it requires a data source or data collection strategy to make it work that compromises your principles.

In any case, you will need to implement a process that can determine what use cases are acceptable. Two artifacts are usually involved in that process:

- A guidance providing a framework for every team involved in the definition of any AI-related product

- A central construct such as committee or board that can evaluate and approve projects that don't clearly meet the criteria specified in the guidance

These criteria should align with your principles and be available transparently. Some typical questions you should ask and properly document about every project are the following:

- Is there any risk of the system causing physical, economical, or emotional damage? For example, a system used to operate a robot among factory workers.

- Will the system be used to deny any consequential services to people? For example, a system used to approve a loan.

- Does the system have any risk of limiting an individual's freedom? For example, a system used to manipulate opinions or cause any kind of deception.

- Is the system limiting user privacy rights? For example, a system that requires sharing sensitive data or using data that was not collected for that purpose.

- Are humans not involved in the decisions made by the system? For example, a system without possibility of human oversight and control mechanisms.

DEVELOPMENT

Even if the use case targeted is aligned with your core principles, the implementation of it may not be. Developers should be aware of the core aspects they need to take into account when developing AI solutions. After the use case is validated and approved, the implementation should also be fully documented as the solution moves through the pipeline in every cycle, from development to operations.

This documentation should identify the steps taken to assure the solution is implemented following the guidelines and provide details on any assumptions made throughout the process, starting with the data being used:

- Is there a clear understanding of how the data was collected, and were the appropriate usages described to the user in that collection?

- What are the limitations of the data being used?

- What are the privacy risks associated with the data, and the mitigation plans?

- How will security access be enforced?

- Is there any influence of past biased behavior in the data?

- Is there any underrepresented population group in the data?

Model development is the core of this stage and a critical component of responsible AI development. As developers create the AI models behind the solution, they should make sure the implementation is aligned with company's principles. For example:

- Can the output provided by the model be explained? Is there any unfair bias observed as a result?

- Are there any known constraints or limitations on the accuracy of the model?

- Is the model vulnerable to AI-specific security attacks? Is it conveniently secured for users with the right access?

- Are third-party models used in the solution aligned with the company's principles?

- Will the model continue to learn with data once deployed? If yes, what are the control mechanisms to avoid potential attacks based on training data?

OPERATIONS

After all of the previous questions have been answered and any problems addressed and the solutions validated, the system can move into production. But even then it needs to be continuously monitored in every development cycle to make sure the initial conditions haven't changed.

For that to be possible, the monitoring process in operations should also include any relevant metrics and regular validation processes to ensure continuing alignment with the initial goals and assumptions. Just as accuracy and performance can degrade in our models, so can fairness and security. And again, we should make sure that we have full traceability so any issues can be resolved quickly and the updated model deployed into production.

Beyond monitoring and assessing the accuracy, performance, bias, and any other potential degradation in our AI systems in production, some other tasks we should perform in the operations cycle are:

- Collecting user feedback or customer satisfaction data to find potential areas that were missed in the design or monitoring of the system

- Providing the right guidance to the operator of the AI system, including how to use it correctly, any limitations of the system, and any maintenance required

- Monitoring and exposing the interpretation of decisions made by the system, to make sure they haven't changed from the design and to help operators understand the recommendations

Practices for the Responsible AI Lifecycle

Infusing responsible AI into the development lifecycle requires the involvement of the entire organization. Some of the most common practices that will help you bootstrap responsible AI are:

Communications
> Company-wide communications prioritizing the importance of responsible AI and describing the processes to manage it

Design standards
> Written policies and guidance for the teams to follow

Training
> Technical and business education focused on responsible AI development

External audits
> Independent audits validating the internal processes and standards

Some tools can be helpful for this purpose, too. If you are using Azure Machine Learning as your solution for MLOps you can use many of its built-in capabilities to manage and enforce responsible AI, for example for bias detection and secure access. You can also set up automatic validation of your responsible AI policies as the AI system moves through the pipeline from development to operations, as well as manual gates that the right owners have to approve during the process (for example, validating the documentation provided).

Finally, think about discussing your responsible AI efforts externally. While your organization should have its own principles, governance systems, and practices to ensure responsible AI development, the conversation should be broader and involve society as a whole.

Collaboration beyond your walls with other enterprises, public organizations, governments, and nonprofits is crucial to ensure that AI can deliver broad benefits. Consider partnering with local and global coalitions and initiatives to help in that transformation. Whether through collaborating with policy makers on regulations for responsible AI, addressing future labor skills with local governments, promoting the development of AI though public programs, or making concrete investments to solve societal challenges, your company can play a helpful role and have a positive impact on your local community and the broader society.

Coming back to Kriti, our AI hero from India, you can understand how important this collaboration is. Kriti knows her work addressing societal challenges can have a strong impact, but it's limited by her ability to scale. That's why she spends a lot of her time working with public institutions that can empower others like her, enabling hundreds or thousands of projects instead of just the ones she can implement herself.

Kriti is a regular collaborator with the UK government, which has launched one of the most comprehensive and ambitious national plans for AI in the world. With this plan, the UK wants to lead the AI revolution, just like it did the first and second industrial revolutions—but having collaborators like Kriti will help the country lead this transformation in a more responsible way. Kriti has testified in front of the House of Lords, advocating for responsible AI, education for the skills of the future, incentives for using AI to solve social problems, and regulations to ensure the ethical development of AI solutions.

Beyond the UK, Kriti is a United Nations Young Leader and provides regular advisory services to its Technology Innovation Lab. She's working on global-scale training programs that will educate the future leaders in human-centric AI around the world.

Think of the impact one person like Kriti can have. She's influencing the AI strategy of an entire country, and shaping activities at a global scale with the UN. By helping regulators, public institutions, and educators, Kriti will scale her work in South Africa and India by a factor of maybe millions.

If one individual like Kriti can have that effect, imagine how helpful your organization can be. AI core principles shouldn't be developed only within your company's walls. They have to be part of a broader conversation between governments, communities, and other companies. AI is being shaped as you read this book, and it is the responsibility of all of us to make sure it is shaped for the good of society as a whole.

## 9

The AI Heroes

I started this book by discussing how, beyond organizational models, strategies, technologies, and use cases, the true secret behind successful AI organizations is their people—amazing people driven by a culture that empowers them. AI heroes make AI organizations.

But what makes an AI hero? I've wondered about this myself many times. What makes the AI heroes like the ones whose stories I've told in this book special? What do they do differently than the rest of us? What can we learn from them? What do they have in common? The AI heroes I've introduced you to in this book have very diverse backgrounds, education levels, cultural origins, and motivations. To find that common thread, I had to go back to one of my favorite books.

The Alchemist (*https://oreil.ly/AIO_9-1*) by Paulo Coelho is one of the most beautiful books you can read. It tells the story of a Spanish shepherd who has a vision of what the author refers to as his "personal legend." A personal legend is one's mission in life, our ultimate purpose. In the case of the shepherd, his legend was to seek a treasure in the Egyptian pyramids. Without a moment's doubt, he sells his flock of sheep and starts a multiyear journey from the beautiful coast of Andalusia to the pyramids of Egypt through the desert.

The only reason for the shepherd to go on this crazy journey is his sense of purpose. And that's the most important attribute our AI heroes have in common —they all have a purpose, they all found their personal legend. Whether it's saving endangered species, finding the cures for rare diseases, transforming industries, or helping abused women, every single one of our AI heroes had a purpose that they could clearly articulate. They all looked at the companies they worked for as instruments to help them accomplish their purpose, and not the other way around.

Moreover, our Spanish shepherd wasn't alone in his journey—he was helped by the titular alchemist. This legendary character is his spiritual leader in the journey. The alchemist won't get the treasure for the shepherd, but he will inspire our friend and transform him, enabling him to pursue his personal legend by himself.

And that's the second thing AI heroes have in common. The companies they work for empowered them to follow their purpose. A company that wants AI heroes has to understand that the company is the one working for its employees' purpose, and not the other way around. Leaders in AI organizations are alchemists that help others to pursue their personal legends. Like Satya Nadella once said to us employees, "Instead of thinking of you working for Microsoft, think of how Microsoft can work for you." Nothing can compete with a company lifted by its employees pursuing their personal legends.

There's a third and last thing that defines our AI heroes. The journey to the pyramids for the Spanish shepherd was far from being a straight line. From very early on he realized that he had to change himself to be successful in this journey. The first day he set foot on the African continent he was robbed and lost everything he had. Without sheep to take care of anymore, he had to learn a new profession to continue his journey. He also had to learn the language and all the secrets of the desert if he wanted to achieve his personal legend.

The shepherd, like all the AI heroes in this book, realized that the most important factor in his journey to achieve his personal legend was his own transformation. People like these find joy in the journey itself, instead of the destination. They see the accomplishment in the learning opportunity, instead of the final goal. Every AI hero in this book grew in the process of achieving their personal legend by embracing and enjoying change. Julián learned the complex nature of rare diseases without any formal medical training. Cathy had studied accounting, but was motivated to learn about AI because of its ethical implications. Kriti learned from experts and associations helping victims of domestic violence in South Africa. Tanya learned about endangered species from her peers at college.

Not a single one of them complained about that learning journey. Actually, just the opposite. They see the learning opportunity as the most important part of their journey, more valuable than achieving the goal itself. These kinds of people are the living representation of a growth mindset: an attitude to life that means we don't shy away from a challenge because of our limitations. Instead, it encourages us to push harder when we are not prepared. It makes us see difficulties and failures as learning opportunities that help us grow.

There's one AI hero I have waited to mention until the end of this book. Sandra Timón is a young developer whom I had the fortune to meet this past year. She had just finished a degree in software engineering with straight A's and an Extraordinary Award. She's specializing in AI and has worked on several projects already. In one of them, she used AI to optimize the distribution in a bike-sharing system, providing recommendations to users and estimating the demand based on multiple factors, such as weather and local events. She's becoming an expert in bot development, too, and she's working on an internal bot at Microsoft to find the right expert for a given request from a customer. She also collaborates with the banking institution Ibercaja, which works with local farmers to optimize their water consumption by using AI.

Not that it matters, but I forgot to mention that Sandra is blind and deaf. She works at Microsoft as a contractor, and she is the perfect representation of the growth mindset found in an AI hero. Some of these heroes had to learn a new area of knowledge to pursue their goal. Some were required to learn an entire new discipline. After his car accident, Cristian had to relearn nearly all his life skills. But Sandra has had to redefine herself every day of her life.

Sandra has a condition called Wolfram syndrome, a rare degenerative disease that gradually causes diabetes and loss of sight and hearing. At the age of 4 she had 40% vision loss, which had risen to 60% by the age of 6. At around age 12, she discovered she could study by making copies of her materials at a bigger scale. She then learned Braille and began using a computer as her primary learning device. She was always ahead of her disease, even when she also lost her hearing during her teenage years. At college, she used a transmitter for the teacher with a receiver connected to her hearing aid. When that was not enough she learned dactylology, a method for spelling out words onto the hands of a person with deafblindness.

Not once have I heard Sandra complain about her journey. She talks about every step of it with a big smile on her face. She's proud that she was prepared for every difficulty along the way, like she's in a personal race with her disease where she always wins. Sandra's personal legend is to change the world with AI, and every stone her disease throws at her is just another opportunity to beat it again.

The next breakthroughs in AI will come from people like Sandra, Julián, Kriti, Athina, Tanya, Chema, Cristian, and Cathy. In their hands, AI is a new tool to make the world a better place tomorrow than it is today—not because they are special, but because they have a purpose and they are willing to learn whatever's necessary in their journey to achieve it.

If you find your purpose, I'd love to hear it. My personal legend is to find more people willing to change the world with AI and help them as I can. I'm not an AI hero myself, but I'll do my best, even if all I can do is connect you with others or inspire others to help you. You can shoot me an email at *davidcsa@microsoft.com* or DM me on Twitter @davidcsa.

Now go find your pyramids!

AI Crash Course for Business Leaders

I love this TV show in which CEOs spend one day undercover among their employees—*Undercover Boss*. It's fascinating (and fun) to watch how terribly unprepared these CEOs are for the most basic jobs in their own companies. Each episode ends with an all-hands meeting at which the CEO shares what they learned during their time with the employees. In most cases they have eye-opening experiences that help them value their employees more, make better decisions, create new policies, or even understand the overall business better.

Most business leaders I know are already very involved in the main business of their companies. In many cases, they have a long experience in that industry and maybe even started in entry-level jobs. I have to admit I've always loved that in a leader.

My father emigrated from a small agricultural village in Spain to the city to work as a carpenter in the shipyards. He ended up founding and managing a furniture company, but he would always be a carpenter at heart. He loved the fine art of carpentry, and he was passionate about the work done by each of the workers in his company. That profound connection to the business made him unique as a manager. Leaders like my father, who are born into an industry and have a deep knowledge of their domain, are passionate about the products they deliver; they inspire and motivate the team, and they develop a natural strategic way of thinking that's impossible to beat.

But something has changed. As we discussed earlier in this book, furniture companies are not just furniture companies anymore—neither are banks, retailers, or shipyards. Every company is now also a software company, and soon enough they will become AI companies. Business leaders of these companies are facing the risk of losing the connection with that critical component in their organizations. Without a foundational understanding of the core concepts involved in that other side of their businesses, they will lack the empathy, leadership, and strategic thinking needed in this new world.

Luckily, I don't think leaders need to have a PhD in data science to keep their jobs in the future. Like those CEOs in *Undercover Boss*, you may need just one day in the life of an AI developer, experiencing the basic techniques firsthand and gaining an understanding of the key concepts behind the job.

In this appendix you will get a high-level overview of a selection of AI technologies. I encourage you to follow the explanations and replicate the examples by yourself, on your own computer.

Welcome to your very own *Undercover Boss: Technical Edition*!

Creating Your First Python Application

Before you start creating your first AI examples, you will need to understand the very basics of programming. You will use a programming language to do anything meaningful with AI, like consuming a service, transforming data, or training your algorithm.

If you already know a programming language, chances are you can use it to create AI applications. I'm a huge fan of C#, and I use it for everything—from web applications, to mobile applications, to cloud services. C# is an amazing language that combines productivity with performance and maintainability, and it also supports all current AI techniques.

However, I'm going to use Python in this book. Python is the most popular language for AI applications today, it is very easy to get started with, and it has many treats for data-intense applications like the ones usually involved with AI.

INSTALLING THE DEVELOPMENT ENVIRONMENT

Before you create your first Python application, make your life easier and download a development environment. These days, the most popular environment for Python is Visual Studio Code. As I mentioned in the Preface of this book, I'm probably about as connected to Visual Studio as my father was to carpentry, so that's an easy choice for me. If you want to try other environments, check out PyCharm, PyDev, or the popular Jupyter Notebook, which provides an interactive way of writing Python code.

To install Visual Studio Code, just go to the website (*https://oreil.ly/AIO_A-1*) and click the Download button. It's available for most operating systems, and no special requirements are needed.

You will also need a Python interpreter installed on your machine. The easiest way to do that is to visit the Python website (*https://oreil.ly/AIO_A-2*) and click the default Download button. You can also download a specific version of Python; this book is based on version 3.6.8, so you may want to download that same version. The installer is straightforward, but make sure you select the option to add Python to your system path. Figure A-1 shows a screenshot of the Windows installer for your reference, with that option checked.

Figure A-1. Installing Python

You're almost there! Now open Visual Studio Code to set it up for your first Python application. Go to File→Preferences→Extensions, and search for the extension "Python." The first one in the list will be the official Python extension provided by Microsoft (Figure A-2); click Install and you're good to go!

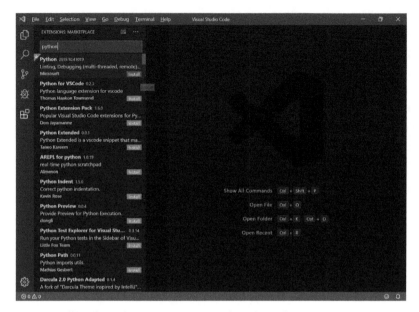

Figure A-2. Installing the Python extension in Visual Studio Code

PYTHON FUNDAMENTALS

You're now ready to create your very first Python application. Select File→New file (or press Ctrl-N) and write the following line of code in the Visual Studio Code editor:

```
print("Hello world")
```

Save the file by selecting File→Save (or pressing Ctrl-S), naming it *HelloWorld.py*. The file will immediately be recognized as a Python file, with the editor highlighting the syntax. You may see a message recommending the installation of a linter. Linters provide real-time feedback on errors and problems in your code as you type, so their use is highly recommended.

You are now ready to run this application. Right-click anywhere in the source editor and select "Run Python File in Terminal." Visual Studio Code will invoke the Python interpreter automatically from the embedded Terminal window, and you will be able to see the result of the execution, as shown in Figure A-3.

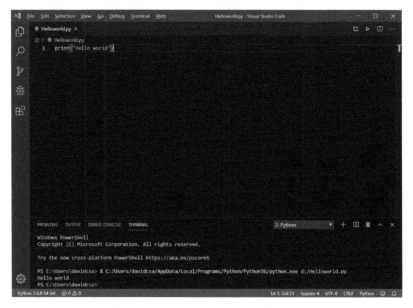

Figure A-3. Your first "Hello world"

Python, like any other programming language out there, supports the concept of variables which can store information under a name. In the case of Python, you don't need to do anything special to use a variable; just initialize it with the = sign. The following code produces the same result as before:

```
text = "Hello world"
print(text)
```

In this case the variable is of type string. Python also supports multiple types of numbers, such as int, float, Decimal, and Fraction. A special type that you will use a lot to store data is the list. Python has rich support for lists, making it great for data manipulation:

```
squares = [1, 4, 9, 16, 25]
print(squares[0])   # First item: 1
print(squares[-2])  # Second item from the end: 16
print(squares[2:4]) # Slicing: [9, 16]
```

The symbol # allows you to write comments in the code. In this case we are using the built-in function print to write a value on the screen, but most times you will use functions that are coming from non-built-in packages, which you can use with the keyword import. However, you will need to install these packages first. For example, this code uses Matplotlib, a very popular package for 2D plotting:

```
import matplotlib.pyplot as plt
import numpy as np

x = np.linspace(0, 20, 100)   # Create a list of evenly spaced numbers
plt.plot(x, np.sin(x))        # Plot the sine of each point
plt.show()                    # Display the plot
```

But if you execute it, you will get an error because the package is not yet installed on your system. Click the Terminal window and type this command:

```
python -m pip install matplotlib
```

Pip is the package installer for Python and allows you to download external packages with additional capabilities. In this case we are installing the package matplotlib (which also installs numpy as a dependency). Depending on the permissions you are running with, you could get an error when executing this command. To avoid this issue, you can install the packages just to your user account by using the --user option:

```
python -m pip install --user matplotlib
```

Alternatively, if you want to install the package for all users of your computer you will need to run the command with elevated privileges:

- If you are using Windows, close Visual Studio Code and launch it again, this time right-clicking it and then selecting "Run as administrator."

- If you are using macOS or Linux, you can elevate your permissions when executing the command by appending sudo to it:

```
sudo python -m pip install matplotlib
```

Matplotlib is very useful for visualizing data. If you run the program again after downloading and installing all the dependencies, you'll see the chart in Figure A-4 on your screen.

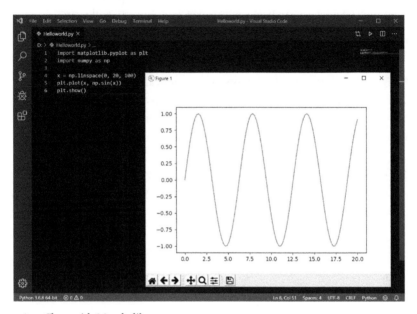

Figure A-4. Chart with Matplotlib

LEARN MORE

This short introduction should be enough for you to follow along with the AI examples in this chapter. If you want to learn more about Python, here are some recommendations of free resources to check out:

- The Python Tutorial (*https://oreil.ly/AIO_A-3*) in the official Python documentation is a great place to start.

- LearnPython.org (*https://oreil.ly/AIO_A-4*) offers a great variety of basic to advanced tutorials, including interactive exercises that can be run directly in the browser.

- The Python reference (*https://oreil.ly/AIO_A-5*) contains all the documentation for the language and libraries.

Consuming Your First AI Service

The easiest and quickest way of infusing AI into an application is to consume a prebuilt AI service. In the case of Azure, these services are called Cognitive Services, and they span areas such as vision, speech, language, and search.

CONFIGURING THE SERVICE

Let's create a simple application that uses a vision service. Before you start, you need to get the information that allows your application to connect to the service. Usually you would do that by creating a Cognitive Services resource in your Azure subscription's portal, but let's assume that you don't have one. You can get a temporary key to use Cognitive Services by following these steps:

1. Go to *http://azure.microsoft.com/en-us/try/cognitive-services* and then click Get API Key (see Figure A-5). In this case, you're going to get a key for Computer Vision.

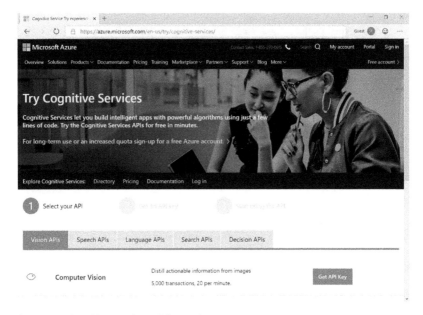

Figure A-5. Cognitive Services trial experience

2. This takes you to a screen with several pricing options. Select Guest to obtain a free trial, and then choose your country.

3. Sign in with one of the supported authentication methods, such as a Microsoft, GitHub, Facebook, or LinkedIn account.

You should get to a similar screen to the one shown in Figure A-6.

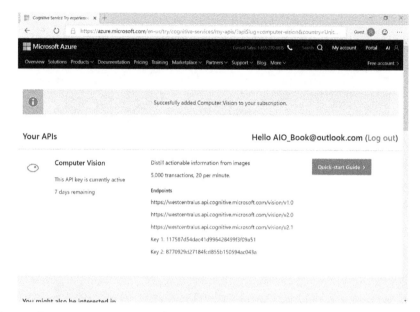

Figure A-6. Computer Vision trial information

Don't close this screen; you'll need the data listed here later.

CONSUMING THE SERVICE FROM PYTHON

Now that you've created your own instance of the vision service, you need to create a new Python file, just like you learned to do in the previous section. You can call it *CognitiveServiceClient.py*. To make things easier, Cognitive Services provides an SDK that you can call directly from your Python code. The SDK for Computer Vision is available in a Python package called `azure-cognitiveservices-vision-computervision`. You also know how to install a package now—just click the Terminal window in Visual Studio Code and type the following:

```
python -m pip install azure-cognitiveservices-vision-computervision
```

You're ready to code! First, import some types you'll need from the package you just installed. Add this code to the beginning of your Python file:

```
from azure.cognitiveservices.vision.computervision \
    import ComputerVisionClient
from azure.cognitiveservices.vision.computervision.models \
    import VisualFeatureTypes
from msrest.authentication import CognitiveServicesCredentials
```

Now try creating a couple of variables with your new Cognitive Service. Replace the value for the ENDPOINT variable shown here with the URL domain listed in the Endpoints section of the Cognitive Services screen you kept open from the previous step, and then replace the KEY value with one of the two keys listed there:

```
ENDPOINT = "https://westcentralus.api.cognitive.microsoft.com"
KEY = "117587d54dac41d996428499f3f09a51"

# Create client
credentials = CognitiveServicesCredentials(KEY)
client = ComputerVisionClient(ENDPOINT, credentials)
```

Now that you have a connection to your service, you just need to call any of the methods of your client and have fun with the results:

```
# Analyze image
url = ("https://upload.wikimedia.org/wikipedia/commons/thumb/1/12/" \
       "Broadway_and_Times_Square_by_night.jpg/450px-Broadway_and_" \
       "Times_Square_by_night.jpg")
image_analysis = client.analyze_image(url,
           visual_features=[VisualFeatureTypes.tags])


# Print analyzed tags
for tag in image_analysis.tags:
    print(tag.name)
```

In this case, I've used an image of a busy street in New York City from Wikipedia (Figure A-7), but you can use any image you like—try searching for objects in a search engine to have some fun!

Figure A-7. The picture used in the example

The resulting tags you will see as an output (Figure A-8) are ordered by level of confidence, and in this case they're pretty accurate: *skyscraper, building, outdoor, light, street, downtown,* and more.

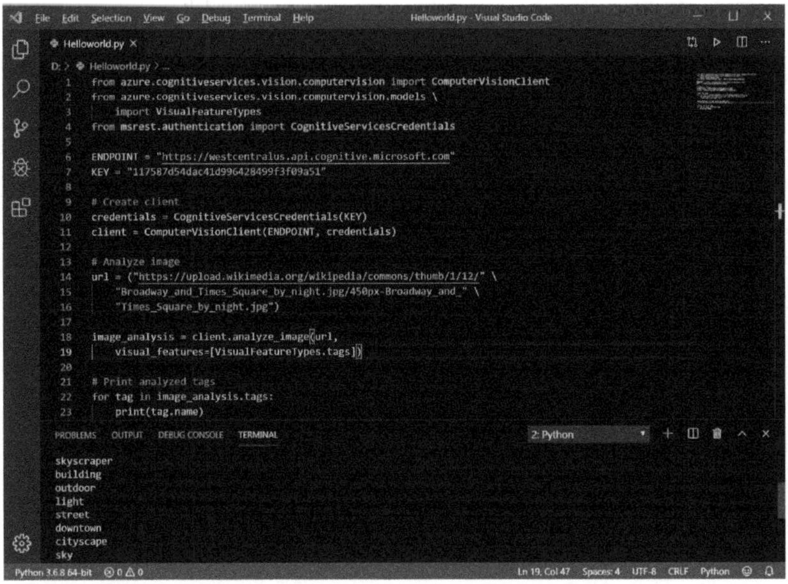

Figure A-8. Calling a vision service

You can explore many other capabilities of the vision service. For example, add the following piece of code to the previous program to get a caption describing the picture:

```
description = client.describe_image(url)
for caption in description.captions:
    print(caption.text)
```

The output will be the following (not bad, right?):

```
a group of people on a city street at night
```

USING TEXT ANALYTICS

You can follow very similar steps to call any of the other Cognitive Services in Azure. Let's try Text Analytics, for example. First, go to the same trial page (*https://oreil.ly/AIO_A-6*) shown in Figure A-5. Click the Language APIs tab on that page, and request an API key for Text Analytics. Follow the same process that you followed with Computer Vision to get the endpoint and key for a Text Analytics instance, as shown in Figure A-9.

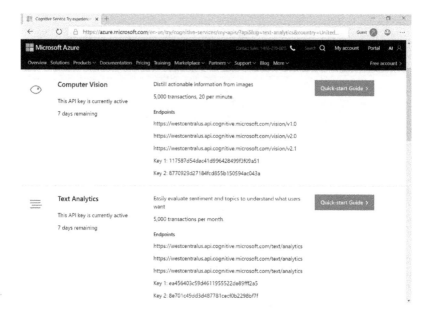

Figure A-9. Text Analytics configuration

Now you can go back to Visual Studio Code and use this new service. First, install the package for the service by running pip in the Terminal window:

```
python -m pip install azure-cognitiveservices-language-textanalytics
```

You will need to change the import clauses in your file to get the TextAnalyticsClient class instead, as well as replacing the key with the new one you just created:

```
from azure.cognitiveservices.language.textanalytics \
import TextAnalyticsClient
from msrest.authentication import CognitiveServicesCredentials

ENDPOINT = "https://westcentralus.api.cognitive.microsoft.com"
KEY = "ea456403c59d4611955522de89fff2a5"
```

Creating the client is extremely similar to the vision example:

```
# Create client
credentials = CognitiveServicesCredentials(KEY)
client = TextAnalyticsClient(ENDPOINT, credentials)
```

You're now ready to call the service. To do that, ask the user for a piece of text to analyze:

```
text = input("Enter a sentence:")
while (text != ""):
    documents = [{
            'id': 0,
            'text': text
        }]

    response = client.sentiment(None, documents)
    print("Sentiment score: " + (str)(response.documents[0].score))
    text = input("Enter a sentence:")
```

You can have some fun writing different sentences. These are the ones that I wrote, with very accurate sentiment scoring (high is positive sentiment, low is negative sentiment):

```
Enter a sentence:I love bread
Sentiment score: 0.9685903191566467
Enter a sentence:I hate cheese
Sentiment score: 0.012747079133987427
Enter a sentence:Yesterday was a waste of time
Sentiment score: 0.09043726325035095
```

LEARN MORE

There are many more Cognitive Services that are as simple to use as the ones you have just seen, in areas such as vision, speech, language, knowledge, decisions, and search. Here are some pointers to resources that will help you get started with them:

- You can explore all the Cognitive Services from the Cognitive Services page (*https://oreil.ly/AIO_A-7*) on the Azure website.

- In the documentation (*https://oreil.ly/AIO_A-8*), you'll find Cognitive Services quickstarts, step-by-step tutorials, and more.

- You can also download the Python samples (*https://oreil.ly/AIO_A-9*) for Cognitive Services.

Creating Your First Bot

One of the services included in Cognitive Services is called Language Understanding, or LUIS. It provides the foundation for conversational AI experiences. LUIS is able to understand a piece of text and convert it into the core intent of the user and the entities involved. For example, if the user says "I want a flight to New York," LUIS will be able to identify that the intent is to buy a plane ticket, and the destination entity is "New York."

Identifying the intent and entities involved in a command is the first step you will do in most bots. With that information your application can decide what to do next, such as asking another question to continue the dialog or performing an action like purchasing a ticket for the user.

CREATING YOUR FIRST LUIS SERVICE

Just like the Computer Vision and Text Analytics services you saw in the previous section, you can create a LUIS service in your Azure account from the Azure portal. I'll assume again that you don't have an Azure account, so let's take a look at how to create a basic LUIS application without one.

Go to the LUIS website (*https://oreil.ly/AIO_A-10*) and sign in with a Microsoft account, or create one if you don't have one. After signing in, you are asked to select your country and accept the terms of service. Optionally, you will be asked to create an Azure resource or you can just use a trial key for 3 months. That takes you to the welcome screen, where you can click "Create a LUIS app now."

You will see a screen listing all your LUIS applications, as shown in Figure A-10.

Figure A-10. LUIS applications

To create your first application, click "Create new app" and pick a name for it (for example, Flight Bot). An assistant will show up. Let's close it for now and go directly to the option BUILD, which takes you to the Intents management screen, shown in Figure A-11.

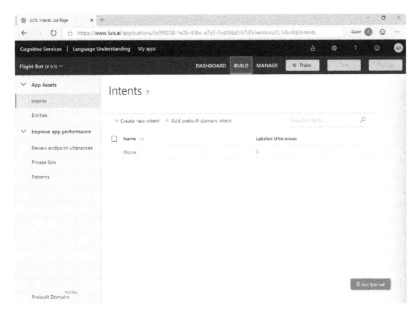

Figure A-11. Intents screen

ADDING INTENTS

Creating a new intent is simple: just click "Create new intent," enter a name for your intent (for example, "Deals"), and type some examples of what the user may say to trigger that intent. Each example is called an *utterance*, and adding these will give more flexibility to your bot. In this example, I've added five utterances to define the intent of getting information about deals (Figure A-12).

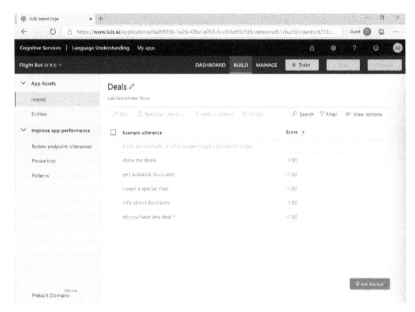

Figure A-12. Utterances for an intent

Before testing this simple application, you have to train the underlying model. Click the Train button and wait for the training to be completed. After it's done you can click the Test button to see how the system is working, as shown in Figure A-13.

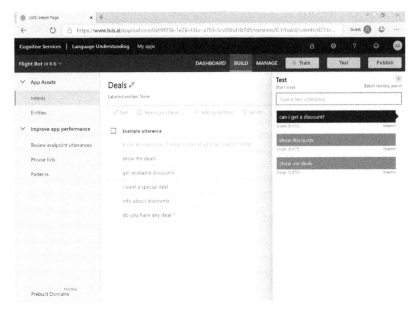

Figure A-13. Testing the intent

In this case we have only one intent, so it is very easy for LUIS to identify it. Still, you can play with different commands and check how the scoring changes depending on the words you use. LUIS uses natural language processing to match the commands with intents, so you don't have to use exactly the same words and the same structure as the sample utterances to get a good match. For example, the sentence "Can I get a discount?" is not listed exactly like that in our utterances but it gets a very high matching score (0.916).

ADDING ENTITIES

Let's add one more intent to make our bot more interesting. In this case we want to add the ability to buy a plane ticket. Buying a ticket is more complex than asking about deals: it involves *entities*. For example, you need to understand the destination of the flight and the date when the user wants to travel. You can define these entities by selecting the option Entities in the left bar in LUIS. After you get to the Entities screen, just click "Create new entity." A dialog box opens, as shown in Figure A-14.

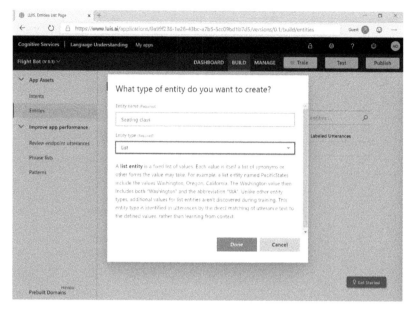

Figure A-14. Creating a new entity

LUIS supports multiple types of entities, like simple terms, hierarchical structures, and composite concepts. In our case we are going to create a Seating Class entity, which is a simple list of options.

Once you create the Seating Class entity you can add items to it. Let's add just two items: *economy* and *business*. For each item you can add synonyms like *coach* or *premium*, or you can even have LUIS recommend additional words by clicking the Recommend option, as shown in Figure A-15.

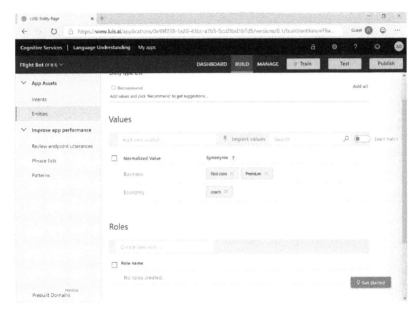

Figure A-15. Creating the entity Seating Class

LUIS also provides prebuilt entities that you can use out of the box. To use them you just need to click "Add prebuilt entity" on the Entities screen. Add two of them now: *datetime* and *geography*, which will get the date for the flight and the destination.

Now that you have all the entities you need, go back to the Intents screen and add a new one. Call this intent Flights, and add some utterances to it like "I want a flight to Paris in coach for tomorrow" and "Business ticket to New York next Tuesday." You can see the result in Figure A-16.

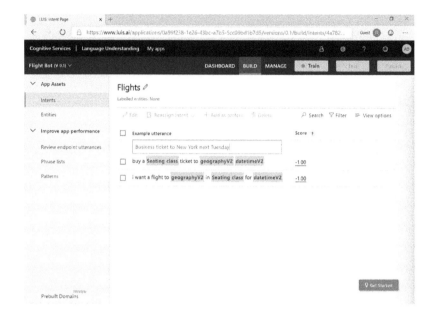

Figure A-16. Creating a Flights intent

As you add the utterances, LUIS automatically detects the entities, replacing them with placeholders. For example, it identifies "Paris" as a geography and it replaces it with the placeholder "geography." You can also do this manually by clicking one or several words in the utterance and selecting an entity from the pop-up menu.

TESTING AND PUBLISHING YOUR SERVICE

Now you're ready to try out your service, which you can do by clicking the Train button. Try some commands first to see how well the system is distinguishing between the two intents. For example, you can try "Show me discounts" and "Get a coach ticket to Paris next Tuesday." You can also test how accurately the system is identifying the entities in the latter example by clicking Inspect. You will see a new panel showing all the entities—Seating Class, datetime, and geography—correctly identified (Figure A-17).

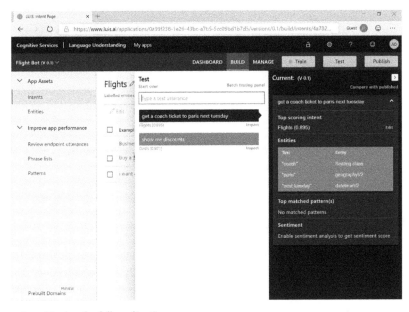

Figure A-17. Testing the full application

When you are happy with the way your project is working, it's time to publish it so that you can consume it from an actual application. Click the Publish button and then select the production environment, as shown in Figure A-18.

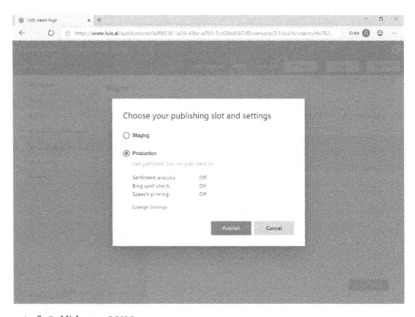

Figure A-18. Publish your LUIS app

This will create a service endpoint in the cloud that you can now call from a bot. In our case, we are going to build a very simple Python application that will act as a bot.

CONSUMING THE SERVICE FROM PYTHON

Go back to Visual Studio Code and install the Python package for LUIS, just like you did for the packages you used earlier:

```
python -m pip install azure-cognitiveservices-language-luis
```

Then, write the following code in Visual Studio Code. Note that you will need to replace the ENDPOINT, KEY, and APPID values shown here with your own values, which you can get by clicking on the MANAGE option in your LUIS application (your endpoint and key will be available on the Azure Resources screen, while the AppID can be found on the "Application Information" screen):

```
from azure.cognitiveservices.language.luts.runtime import LUISRuntimeClient
from msrest.authentication import CognitiveServicesCredentials

ENDPOINT = "https://westus.api.cognitive.microsoft.com"
KEY = "ea841e078bb44a6db92629338d3d322c"
APPID = "0a99f238-1e26-43bc-a7b5-5cc09bd1b7d5"

# Create client
credentials = CognitiveServicesCredentials(KEY)
client = LUISRuntimeClient(ENDPOINT, credentials)

text = input("Enter a sentence:")
while (text != ""):
    result = client.prediction.resolve(
            APPID,
            text
        )
    print(result.top_scoring_intent.intent)

    for entity in result.entities:
            print("\t-> Entity {} ({})".format(entity.entity, entity.type))
    text = input("Enter a sentence:")
```

The code for your first bot is very simple. It just reads your input and calls your LUIS endpoint with that text. Then, it prints the detected intent and any entities to the screen. Try using new sentences to test your bot. Here are some examples:

```
Enter a sentence: I want a deal
Deals
Enter a sentence: business ticket to Atlanta on July 25th
Flights
            -> Entity july 25th (builtin.datetimeV2.date)
            -> Entity atlanta (builtin.geographyV2.city)
            -> Entity business (Seating Class)
```

In a real bot, your code will do something with the intents detected and the entities extracted. For example, it might connect to a backend to actually find a flight with that information, or it might ask the user additional questions in a dialogue.

A real bot will also be available in conversational channels like Skype, Facebook Messenger, and Slack, and it may have additional capabilities like authentication, analytics, or automatic translation. Fortunately, you don't have to build all those capabilities by yourself; there are libraries and tools available that provide the plumbing for all of that.

Bot Framework (*https://oreil.ly/AIO_A-11*) is an example of such a tool. You can use Bot Framework to easily create bots that you can host anywhere. Azure Bot Service (*https://oreil.ly/AIO_A-12*) is a managed service based on Bot Framework that you can use to easily create a bot in the cloud. Using Azure Bot Service in combination with Cognitive Services will enable you to create powerful bots like the omni-bots and omni-channel bots you learned about in Chapter 2.

LEARN MORE

If you want to create more advanced bots, here are a few ideas for next steps:

- Create an Azure-based bot with Azure Bot Service (*https://oreil.ly/AIO_A-13*).

- Create a question-and-answer bot based on documents and FAQs with the QnA Maker service (*https://oreil.ly/AIO_A-14*).

- Learn about the templates and solutions available for Bot Framework (*https://oreil.ly/AIO_A-15*), such as the Virtual Assistant and Enterprise templates.

Creating Your First Machine Learning Model

So far, you have been using prepackaged AI models that are available in the cloud. In some cases, like with LUIS, you have also customized the model under the hood for your own scenario, but you didn't have to create it yourself. In this section, you are going to learn how to create an AI model from scratch.

BASIC CONCEPTS

If you think about it, a model like the ones you have been using performs a very simple operation: it transforms an input into an output by applying a certain function. Using math notation, a model can be represented like this:

$$\hat{y} = h(x)$$

where:

- x is the input for our model. It could be just a number, or, more commonly, it could be a series of numbers, also known as a *vector*. For example, it could be the average income in a neighborhood or the intensity of every pixel in an image.

- $\hat{y}$ is the output for our model, also known as the *predicted value*. It could either be a number, like the estimated price of a house, or a discrete set of categories, like the objects detected in a picture. The first case is called a *regression*, and the second case is called a *classification*.

- h is the function that transforms the input into the output. It's referred to as the *hypothesis function* or the *model*, because it represents a hypothesis that models how the reality works.

Our work as AI developers is to find the best function h for our scenario. For example, it could transform the average income in a neighborhood to the estimated price of a house, or it could output the identified object category from an input of an image.

The magic of machine learning is that we don't need to know what the real function is. Instead, let's create a function that mimics the real one by using examples of pairs of inputs with the corresponding outputs. Those pairs are known as *training data* or *labeled data*, or just the *dataset*.

For example, the following code loads a well-known diabetes dataset:

```
from sklearn import datasets

dataset = datasets.load_diabetes()
print(dataset.feature_names)
```

Scikit-learn (sklearn) is the most popular machine learning package for Python. It comes with many sample datasets that you can use to learn the basic techniques of machine learning. In this case we are loading a sample dataset containing data from more than 400 patients with diabetes. The input data contains 10 fields for each patient with several data points, also called *features*. The preceding code prints the names of each of the 10 features, which include patient data such as age and body mass index, and six blood serum measurements:

```
['age', 'sex', 'bmi', 'bp', 's1', 's2', 's3', 's4', 's5', 's6']
```

The data itself is provided in the field data. Add these two lines of code to see its content:

```
print(dataset.data.shape)
print(dataset.data)
```

The data field is a matrix with 442 rows and 10 columns, as shown by the operation shape. Each row contains the data for a patient (442 in total), and each column corresponds to a feature (10 in total). The datasets provided by scikit-learn are *normalized* (i.e., changed to a common scale) to make them easier to manage; that's why the age shows up as a very small number:

```
['age', 'sex', 'bmi', 'bp', 's1', 's2', 's3', 's4', 's5', 's6']
(442, 10)
[[ 0.03807591 0.05068012 0.06169621 ...  0.01990842 -0.01764613]
 [-0.00188202 -0.04464164 -0.05147406 ... -0.06832974 -0.09220405]
 ...
 [-0.04547248 -0.04464164 -0.0730303 ... -0.00421986 0.00306441]]
```

The diabetes dataset also contains an *output* or *target* metric, which in this case represents an indication of disease progression after one year. It is also a vector of 442 elements, one for each patient. Add the following statement to the program:

```
print(dataset.target)
```

The result will show the target vector:

```
[151.  75. 141. 206. 135.  97. 138.  63. 110. 310. 101.  69. 179. 185.
 ...
  49.  64.  48. 178. 104. 132. 220.  57.]
```

LINEAR REGRESSION

It's time to create our first machine learning model. Imagine that you want to predict the diabetes progression in a patient. To simplify things, let's also imagine you only know the patient's body mass index (BMI). Your goal is to find a function *h* that models the transformation between the BMI of a patient and their diabetes progression. The following code shows a chart (Figure A-19) with all the training data you have available for BMI and disease progression pairs:

```
from sklearn import datasets
import matplotlib.pyplot as plt
```

```
dataset = datasets.load_diabetes()

x = dataset.data[:,2] # BMI is the feature with index 2
y = dataset.target

plt.scatter(x,y)
plt.show()
```

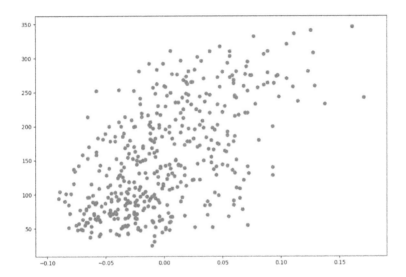

Figure A-19. BMI and diabetes progression

A very simple way of modeling that transformation is by assuming it's a straight line. That technique is called a *linear regression*, and it's like the "Hello, World" of machine learning. The hypotheses function *h* in this case is as simple as this:

$$h(x) = \theta_0 + \theta_1 \cdot x_1 + \theta_2 \cdot x_2 + ... + \theta_n \cdot x_n$$

where x_1 to x_n are the input features and θ_0 to θ_n are the parameters of the model, which simply apply a weight to each of the inputs. Figure A-20 shows a linear regression for a very simple case in which we have only four pairs of inputs and outputs.

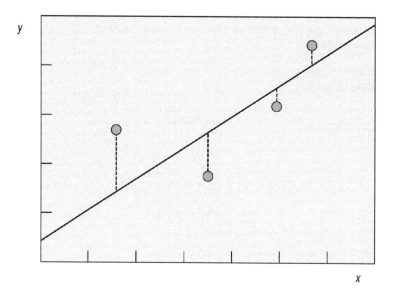

Figure A-20. Linear regression

Our points will not be aligned in a straight line. The difference between a real output and the corresponding prediction of our function is called the *error*, and it's represented with dashed lines in Figure A-20.

To evaluate how big the combined error is, we will also have to define a *loss function* or *cost function*. The most common loss function for regression is called *mean squared error* (MSE), and it's basically the sum of squared errors for all the points. Using MSE as our loss function has several advantages. For example, it will try to avoid points that are far from our hypothesis function. Another advantage is that there is a *closed-form solution* to find that line, which means we can calculate the line using a mathematical equation that gives the result directly. That equation is called the *normal equation*, and fortunately for you you won't need to learn it because it's already implemented in scikit-learn. To use it, just add an `import` statement in the previous file:

```
from sklearn import linear_model
```

Then, replace the code you had before to plot the data with this version:

```
x = x.reshape(-1,1) # Linear regression requires a matrix
regr = linear_model.LinearRegression()
regr.fit(x, y)
```

The regr object now contains a trained linear regression model. Let's test it with three BMI values:

```
# Predict the progression of three different BMI values
new_x = [[-0.1], [0], [0.2]]
predicted_y = regr.predict(new_x)
print(predicted_y)
```

The predicted values will show up on the screen:

```
[ 57.18995812 152.13348416 342.02053624]
```

Let's visualize these results in a chart to see them better:

```
# Visualize results in chart
plt.plot(new_x, predicted_y, color = 'black', linewidth=3)
plt.scatter(x, y, color = 'blue')
plt.show()
```

Figure A-21 shows the result, a line that follows the overall trend of the training data.

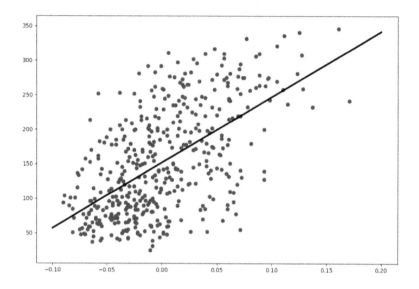

Figure A-21. Linear regression for BMI and diabetes progression

MULTIVARIABLE LINEAR REGRESSION

The previous example was especially simple because we assumed the output (diabetes progression) was dependent on only one scalar input (BMI). In real life things won't be as simple, and outputs will depend on several inputs. The good news is that the linear regression technique also works for multivariable features with almost no modifications.

The previous code doesn't need to be changed much to calculate a linear regression where all 10 features are used in the model:

```
dataset = datasets.load_diabetes()
x = dataset.data
y = dataset.target
print(x.shape) # Shows (442,10)

regr = linear_model.LinearRegression()
regr.fit(x, y)

# Predict the progression of a patient
new_x = [[0, 0, 0, 0, 0, 0, 0, 0, 0, 0]]
predicted_y = regr.predict(new_x)
print(predicted_y) # Shows prediction [152.13348416]
```

GRADIENT DESCENT

We were very lucky with the linear regression. A closed-form solution was possible, allowing us to get the optimal parameters for our model just by solving an equation. However, more complex machine learning algorithms don't have closed-form solutions. And even in the case of a linear regression, the closed-form solution is often not practical to use because it gets very inefficient when you have a large number of features.

For those cases, you will use a technique called *gradient descent*. The general idea of the gradient descent is to tweak the parameters of the model iteratively in order to minimize the loss function. The concept is similar to climbing down a mountain without knowing the way down. A good strategy is to always go down, following the direction with the highest negative slope. Figure A-22 shows that concept for training a machine learning model. At each step we calculate the trend for the loss function (or, in mathematical terms, the partial derivative of the loss function). Then we move in that direction for a new point, and we repeat the process until we get close to the minimum value for the loss function. In this case, we are assuming that our machine learning model has two parameters, which is very convenient for visualizing in a chart. However, in real life a model will need to learn many more parameters. The color represents the value of the loss function for that particular combination of parameters.

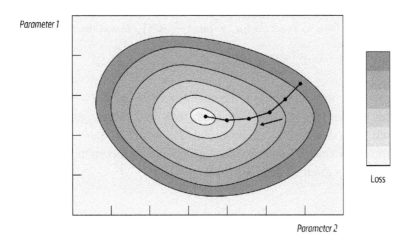

Figure A-22. Gradient descent for two parameters

You will use gradient descent or a variation of it for training most of your machine learning models. In the case of the linear regression algorithm, you can use the SGDRegressor class in scikit-learn to do all of the work for you. The SGDRegressor class implements a variation of gradient descent called *stochastic gradient descent*, which is more efficient because the direction of the change is calculated using just one training value at a time, instead of using the entire training set in every step. You can control the behavior of it in great detail, but in this case we will just modify the number of steps to see the convergence in a chart:

```python
import matplotlib.pyplot as plt
from sklearn import datasets
from sklearn import linear_model

dataset = datasets.load_diabetes()
x = dataset.data[:,2]
y = dataset.target

x = x.reshape(-1,1)

n_iter = [100, 1000, 5000, 20000]
colors = ["#cccccc", "#888888", "#444444", "#000000"]
new_x = [[-0.1], [0], [0.2]]

for i, n in enumerate(n_iter):
    regr = linear_model.SGDRegressor(max_iter=n)
    regr.fit(x, y)
    predicted_y = regr.predict(new_x)
    plt.plot(new_x, predicted_y, color=colors[i], linewidth=3)

plt.scatter(x, y, color = 'blue')
plt.show()
```

To make it more interesting, the code trains the model with four different values for the number of steps (100, 1000, 5000, and 20000), and shows each of the resulting models with a different color. The result is shown in Figure A-23, where you can visualize how the model gets better by increasing the number of iterations using a gradient descent.

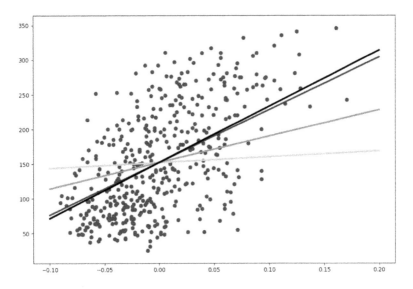

Figure A-23. Gradient descent in action for a linear regression

In these examples we have been estimating the progression of a disease, but you can use the same technique to predict sales forecasts, or the time until a machine will require maintenance, or the expected demand for a given product.

CLASSIFICATION MODELS

So far we've been working with models that output numerical values. Another common set of algorithms are focused on assigning inputs into categories—they are called *classification algorithms*.

To illustrate this concept, we will use another very common dataset that is considered the "Hello, World" for classification. The Iris dataset is based on mor-phological data from three different types of Iris flowers. Four features are part of this dataset: the length and width of the sepals and the petals, in centimeters.

Scikit-learn also provides this dataset with the built-in method load_iris. The following code shows all the flowers that are part of the dataset with their corresponding petal widths and lengths:

```
import matplotlib.pyplot as plt
import matplotlib.colors as colors
from sklearn import datasets

dataset = datasets.load_iris()
x = dataset.data
y = dataset.target

print(dataset.feature_names)

# Draw plot
plt.xlabel('Petal length')
plt.ylabel('Petal width')
cmap = colors.ListedColormap(['red', 'green', 'blue'])
plt.scatter(x[:,2], x[:,3], c=y, cmap=cmap)

# Draw legend
species = [['Setosa', 'red'], ['Versicolor', 'green'], ['Virginica', 'blue']]
for s in species:
    plt.scatter([],[], label=s[0], c=s[1])
plt.legend()

plt.show()
```

The resulting output is shown in Figure A-24, where the three species of flowers are represented with different colors. The goal of our classification task is to identify the species of a new flower, given its characteristics.

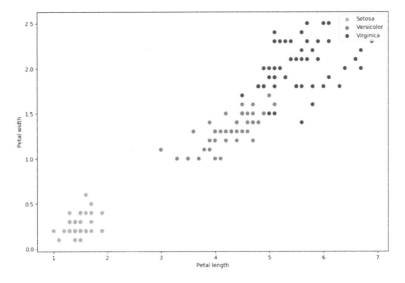

Figure A-24. The Iris dataset

The simplest classification algorithm is *logistic regression*. Don't get confused by that name—logistic regression is a classification algorithm, but it predicts the *probability* of a category, which is a number.

The equation behind a logistic regression is extremely similar to that for a linear regression:

$$h(x) = \sigma(\theta_o + \theta_1 \cdot x_1 + \theta_2 \cdot x_2 + ... + \theta_n \cdot x_n)$$

In fact, it's the same equation, which applies a bias and a weight to each of the inputs, with a logistic function (σ) applied to it. The logistic function—also called the *logit*—is a sigmoid function that outputs a number between 0 and 1 that represents the probability, as shown in Figure A-25.

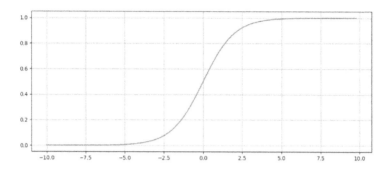

Figure A-25. Sigmoid function

The process for training this model is conceptually very similar to that for the regular linear regression:

1. We define a cost function that will represent the size of the overall error in our trained model.

2. We calculate the partial derivative of that cost function, which will guide our gradient descent to train the model.

In every training iteration, we will evaluate this function to decide which direction to tweak the parameters of the model in. Fortunately again for us, scikit-learn also implements this entire process in a very simple class called `LogisticRegression`.

The following code trains a classification model using this class, and then shows the result visually:

```
import numpy as np
import matplotlib.pyplot as plt
import matplotlib.colors as colors
from sklearn.linear_model import LogisticRegression
from sklearn import datasets

dataset = datasets.load_iris()
x = dataset.data[:, 2:4]  # Use only petal width and length as features
y = dataset.target

# Train a multiclass logistic regression
logreg = LogisticRegression(C=1e5, solver='lbfgs', multi_class='multinomial')
logreg.fit(x, y)
```

```
# Plot the decision boundary
cmap = colors.ListedColormap(['red', 'green', 'blue'])
x_min, x_max = x[:, 0].min() - .5, x[:, 0].max() + .5
y_min, y_max = x[:, 1].min() - .5, x[:, 1].max() + .5
h = .02
xx, yy = np.meshgrid(np.arange(x_min, x_max, h), np.arange(y_min, y_max, h))
z = logreg.predict(np.c_[xx.ravel(), yy.ravel()])
z = z.reshape(xx.shape)
plt.figure(1, figsize=(4, 3))
plt.pcolormesh(xx, yy, z, cmap=cmap)

# Plot the training points
plt.scatter(x[:, 0], x[:, 1], c=y, edgecolors='k', cmap=cmap)
plt.xlabel('Petal length')
plt.ylabel('Petal width')

plt.show()
```

Figure A-26 shows the output of this code.

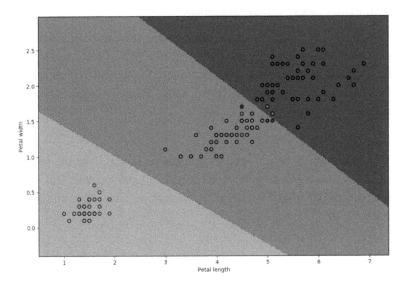

Figure A-26. Logistic regression predictions

The background color in the chart represents the prediction of the model for all the combinations of lengths and widths of the petals. You can see how the algorithm did quite a good job of separating the space into three areas corresponding to each species.

Using this trained model, you can classify any new flower given its characteristics. The method `predict` in the `LogisticRegression` class will return the predicted class of the input. Using `predict_proba` will return the probability of the input belonging to each class. For example, add the following lines to the existing code:

```
new_x = [[5, 1]] # Petal length 5, Petal width 1
predicted = logreg.predict_proba(new_x)
print(predicted)
```

The output will show a high probability (0.9965) for class 1, versicolor:

```
[[4.32151732e-12 9.97649156e-01 2.35084407e-03]]
```

You can easily use the same technique to identify the probability of a customer to churn, or the likelihood of a transaction to be fraudulent, or the chances of an ad being clicked.

OTHER MACHINE LEARNING ALGORITHMS

Linear regression and logistic regression are the two most foundational algorithms in machine learning. In real life, you will use the best algorithm for your scenario, in a mix between science and intuition. We won't cover additional algorithms in detail in this book, but here's a quick rundown on some of the most popular ones:

Polynomial regression

This algorithm is very similar to a linear regression, but the prediction is modeled with a polynomial curve instead of a straight line. It is very useful for describing more complex relationships, like the one shown in Figure A-27.

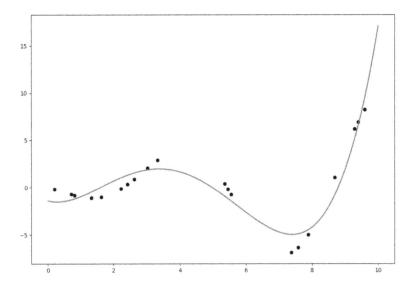

Figure A-27. Polynomial regression

Support vector machines (SVMs)

SVMs are primarily used for classification scenarios. They generally perform better than a logistic regression because they maximize the separation, or margin, between the two classes. SVMs can also perform nonlinear classifications using polynomial, radial, or sigmoid-like functions. Figure A-28 shows the maximized margin in an SVM classification.

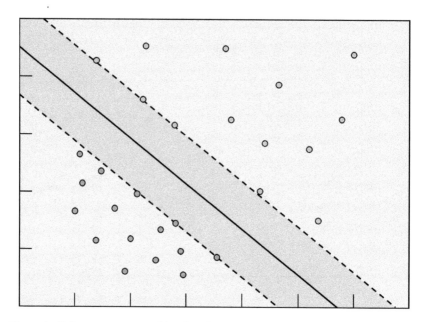

Figure A-28. Support vector machine classification

Naive Bayes classifiers

These classifiers use Bayes' theorem to identify the probability of an instance being of a certain class. Bayes' theorem calculates the probability of a certain event (e.g., the object is an apple) based on conditions related to the event (e.g., weight of the object, color, size, etc.). The resulting equation is one of the most famous in probability theory:

$$P(A|B) = \frac{P(B|A)\,P(A)}{P(B)}$$

where A is the event to predict and B is a condition related to the event.

Decision trees

Both for regression and classification tasks, these algorithms go from observations represented in the branches of a tree to conclusions represented in its leaves. Each fork in the tree is a question that drives the flow through the tree, which makes this algorithm very easy to interpret and transparent. Figure A-29 shows an example of a decision tree used for classification.

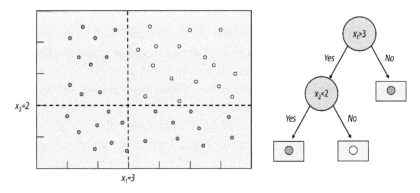

Figure A-29. Decision tree classification

Ensemble models

A common technique to improve the accuracy of any prediction is to combine multiple models in an ensemble. The resulting model will achieve better accuracy than any of the individual models on its own. A simple way of doing this is called *bagging*, in which each model is trained on a subset of the data and then they all vote with equal weight. *Boosting* is a more sophisticated technique in which each model is trained with an emphasis on misclassified instances from previous models. When the individual models are decision trees, you will hear a lot about an ensemble method known as a *random decision forest*. In this technique, a multitude of decision trees are created on a random subset of features, and their predictions are brought together in a combined output.

Creating Your First Artificial Neural Network Model

Neural networks are one of the hottest topics in AI nowadays. At its core, an artificial neural network is just another machine learning algorithm like the ones you saw in the previous section. However, recent advances in neural networks have allowed many breakthrough applications that no other machine learning algorithm has been able to achieve previously.

The mystical nature of neural networks starts with what they use as an inspiration for their structure: the human brain.

ARTIFICIAL NEURAL NETWORKS AND THE HUMAN BRAIN

In 1852, Santiago Ramon y Cajal was born in a small town in the region of Navarra, Spain. He was an artist at heart, but was forced to attend medical school by his father, who never appreciated his artistic talent. Little did he know that, as the stories of many of the AI heroes in this book have proven, innovation always requires science and art in equal doses.

Ramon y Cajal was fascinated by a technique called Golgi's method that could randomly stain some neurons black, leaving the surrounding cells transparent. He used and improved that method to create extensive detailed drawings of neural material from many species, which was so densely intertwined that standard microscope inspection was not feasible. Figure A-30 shows one of those drawings, in this case from a pigeon cerebellum.

The drawings supported Ramon y Cajal's biggest contribution to neuroanatomy: despite what we had thought until then, a brain was not a continuous complex mass, but really a set of much simpler interconnected units called neurons.

Further research by the community, including the work of one of his students, Rafael Lorente, would shed more light on how each of these neurons work. A typical neuron would receive electrochemical signals via filaments called dendrites. Depending on the signal, the neuron will then generate an all-or-nothing pulse through a single output called an axon. The axon connects the neuron to other cells—typically neurons—which then repeat the process. The human brain is in fact a huge network of approximately 100 billion neurons and 100 trillion connections.

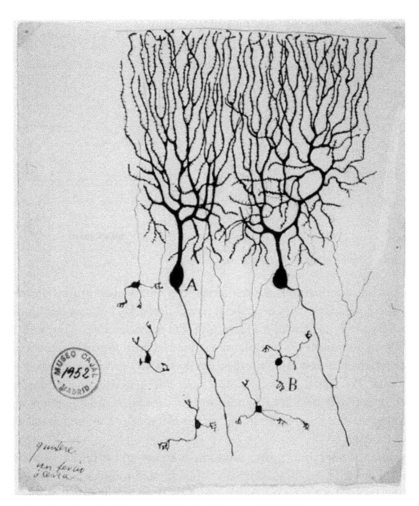

Figure A-30. Drawing of a pigeon cerebellum by Ramon y Cajal, 1899

An *artificial neuron* is loosely based on how an individual neuron works. As shown in Figure A-31, an artificial neuron also takes multiple signals as an input. It applies an activation function to those signals (after applying a weight to each of them) and then outputs the result.

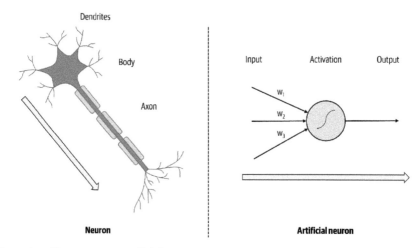

Figure A-31. Neurons versus artificial neurons

These artificial neurons are connected with others in an *artificial neural network*. There are many types of artificial neural networks, but here we'll focus on the simplest one, as shown in Figure A-32: the *feedforward neural network*. With this approach, neurons are grouped into layers and the information moves in just one direction. The first layer is called the *input layer*, and it's connected to the input data. The last layer is the *output layer* and generates the output of our model. In between are a variable number of *hidden layers*. Adding many hidden layers can increase the complexity and power of a model, a technique referred to as *deep learning*.

Similar as they may seem, however, neurons and artificial neurons are actually quite different. Real neurons are much more complex, and there's a lot we don't know about their inner behavior, how they are connected, or how they learn over time. Just like airplanes don't work like birds, artificial neural networks don't work like brains, and they do very different things.

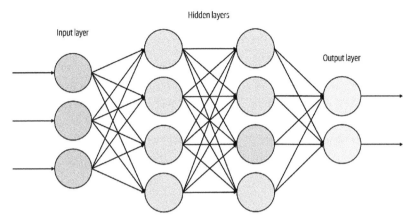

Figure A-32. Feedforward neural network

HOW ARTIFICIAL NEURAL NETWORKS WORK

You already know most of the concepts involved in an artificial neural network. Like any other machine learning algorithm, artificial neural networks define a hypothesis function $h(x)$ that transforms the inputs x into an output y based on trained parameters w, as shown in Figure A-33.

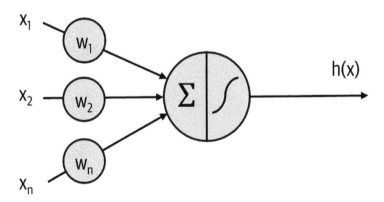

Figure A-33. h(x) in a simple artificial neuron

The hypothesis function first computes a weighted sum of the inputs:

$$z = w_1 \bullet x_1 + w_2 \bullet x_2 + \dots + w_n \bullet x_n$$

and then applies the activation function a:

$$h(x) = a(w_1 \bullet x_1 + w_2 \bullet x_2 + \dots + w_n \bullet x_n)$$

This looks a lot like the logistic regression we saw before. In fact, a logistic regression is a particular case of artificial neuron in which the activation function is a sigmoid. It's more common, however, to use other types of activation functions in artificial neurons, though.

The *ReLU* function (Figure A-34) is the most widely used activation function. It gives an output of x if x is positive and 0 otherwise, with a maximum value of 1.

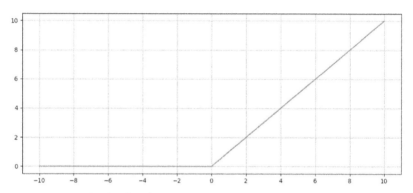

Figure A-34. ReLU activation function

The *tanh* function (Figure A-35) is similar to the sigmoid function but is bound to (–1, 1).

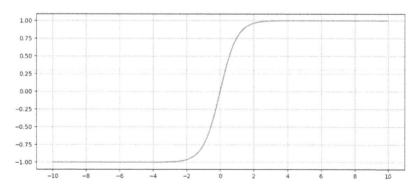

Figure A-35. Tanh activation function

The *softmax* function (Figure A-36) is very similar to a sigmoid, but it divides each output such that the total sum is equal to 1. It's very useful as an output layer because it can provide the probability for each category in a classifier (e.g., an object recognized in an image).

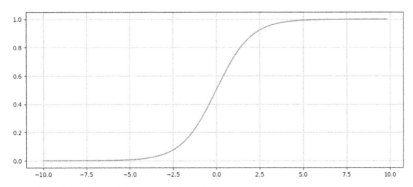

Figure A-36. Softmax sigmoid activation function

These activation functions have another important characteristic in common: they are all differentiable. This means that they are great for training because we can use the gradient descent method we have seen before for traditional machine learning algorithms. The training technique is very similar.

First, we feed a training instance x to each neuron in the input layer, and compute the output. This becomes the input to the next layer, which performs its own computation and passes its output on to the following layer, and so on until the output layer is reached. This stage is called the *forward pass*. Figure A-37 shows this phase for a very simple neural network.

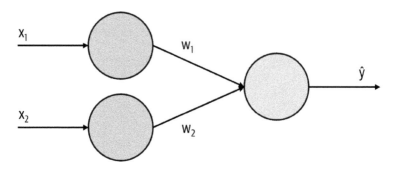

Figure A-37. Forward pass example

In this example, the predicted output ŷ would simply be the result of applying the activation function to the last layer. If we used a sigmoid activation function, it would look something like this:

$$\hat{y} = sigmoid(x_1 \bullet w_1 + x_2 \bullet w_2)$$

We then measure the output error by using our cost function of choice. For regressions, we can use the same cost function we used earlier, the mean squared error. In the previous example we have only one output, so the MSE is very simple to calculate—we just need to square the difference between the real value and the predicted value:

$$e = (y - \hat{y})^2$$

The next phase is the most important one for training a neural network: it's called the *reverse pass*, or *backpropagation*. In this phase we update all the weights in our neural network, learning from the prediction we just made. The first step is to propagate the error back, proportionally to the weights in each neuron, as shown in Figure A-38.

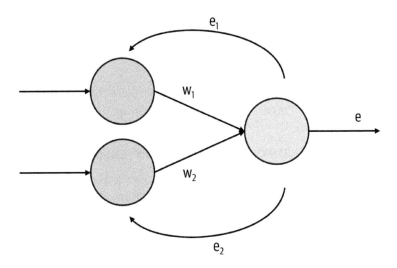

Figure A-38. Error backpropagation

In our simple example the proportions are very easy to calculate because we have only two weights:

$$e_1 = \left(\frac{w_1}{w_1 + w_2}\right) \times e$$

$$e_2 = \left(\frac{w_2}{w_1 + w_2}\right) \times e$$

After we have the errors for every neuron in our network, we tweak the weights in each connection by applying the gradient descent algorithm. The slope is calculated by differentiating the error function, similarly to the gradient descent in any other machine learning algorithm. We won't cover the detailed formula for that slope, but here's what the updated weight will look like:

new w_i = old w_i - a • slope

Following the same example we used before, we want to go "down the mountain" of our cost function, so we take a step in the opposite direction of the slope (that's why we apply a negative increment). a is called the *learning rate*, and it's a parameter we will tune to take bigger or smaller steps down the mountain.

After this step we will have updated all the weights of our neural network to make the output closer to the value of this particular training instance. If we repeat this process for every training instance we have in our dataset and then repeat the whole procedure several times (each one called an *epoch*), we will end up with our first trained artificial neural network.

Fortunately for us, we won't need to apply all these formulas and do these calculations manually. There are plenty of deep learning frameworks that can do all the hard work for us.

CREATING A NEURAL NETWORK WITH KERAS AND TENSORFLOW

The two most popular deep learning frameworks among AI developers nowadays are *TensorFlow* and *Keras*. TensorFlow is what is commonly known as a *backend* framework. These frameworks take care of the complex numerical computation required for deep learning, scaling it efficiently and accelerating it with graphics processing units (GPUs). TensorFlow uses dataflow graphs to describe these computations, with nodes representing the mathematical operations and edges representing multidimensional data arrays called *tensors* on which these operations are performed. TensorFlow is provided as open source and maintained primarily by Google. Other popular backends for deep learning include MXNet (primarily maintained by Amazon), PyTorch (Facebook), and Cognitive Toolkit (Microsoft).

Backend frameworks are low-level and require deep expertise on the math behind neural networks. Because of that, *frontend* frameworks are extremely popular among developers who don't require the level of control needed for research scenarios. The most popular frontend framework is called Keras, and it's available for Python. The beauty of frontend deep learning frameworks like Keras is that they provide a high level of abstraction that allows you to focus on defining the best neural network architecture for your scenario instead of on the math behind it. Under the hood, these frameworks are still using the same backend libraries you can use directly; for example, Keras supports TensorFlow, Cognitive Toolkit, Theano, and MXNet as the backend framework.

Keras is included in the TensorFlow package, so installing both on your machine is as simple as running a `pip` command like the ones you saw earlier:

```
python -m pip install --user tensorflow
```

This command will install the latest version of TensorFlow. You can also install specific versions of TensorFlow, specifically for an operating system or Python version (*https://oreil.ly/AIO_A-16*).

The dataset we will use for our first neural network is called MNIST, and it contains hand-written digits that our model will need to classify correctly. The MNIST dataset is directly available to load as part of the Keras API:

```
import tensorflow as tf
import matplotlib.pyplot as plt
import numpy as np

mnist = tf.keras.datasets.mnist
(x_train, y_train), (x_test, y_test) = mnist.load_data()

print(x_train.shape) # Outputs (60000, 28, 28)
print(x_test.shape) # Outputs (10000, 28, 28)
```

The data is divided into two datasets, one with 60,000 instances called x_train (the training dataset), and another one with 10,000 instances called x_test (the testing dataset). Each instance is represented with a 28 × 28–pixel matrix, where each element is a pixel of the image. To see the first image in the dataset, you can simply use the function imshow of Matplotlib:

```
plt.imshow(x_train[0], cmap='gray')
plt.show()
```

The output is shown in Figure A-39.

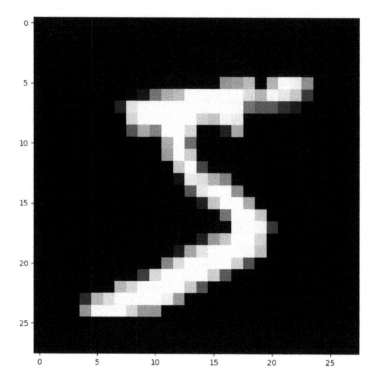

Figure A-39. First instance in the MNIST dataset

Labels are stored in the `y_train` and `y_test` arrays. For example, the following code will provide 5 as an output, which represents the label of the digit shown in the preceding image:

```
print(y_train[0]) # Outputs '5'
```

We are almost ready to design our first neural network. Before we do that, we need to normalize the input. The MNIST dataset is provided with every pixel value between 0 and 255, but we need those values to be between 0 and 1. Fortunately, we just need to use the function `Normalize` provided in Keras to do that:

```
x_train =tf.keras.utils.normalize(x_train, axis=1)
x_test = tf.keras.utils.normalize(x_test, axis=1)
```

Designing a neural network is actually very easy using Keras. The simplest model in Keras is called a *Sequential* model, and it is built by stacking layers sequentially. Every layer is added with an instruction that identifies the type of the layer and some parameters defining the layer, such as the number of nodes and the activation function used in each neuron:

```
model = tf.keras.models.Sequential()
model.add(tf.keras.layers.Flatten())
model.add(tf.keras.layers.Dense(256, activation = tf.nn.relu))
model.add(tf.keras.layers.Dense(256, activation = tf.nn.relu))
model.add(tf.keras.layers.Dense(10, activation = tf.nn.softmax))
```

The artificial neural network we just created has four layers:

- A first layer of type Flatten. This layer performs a very basic transformation that turns a bidimensional entry (28 elements by 28 elements in our case) into a one-dimensional entry of 784 elements (28 × 28), which is what our neural network is expecting.

- A second layer of type Dense. A dense layer is basically a set of neurons that are fully connected with the previous layer, so every neuron in this layer has a weighted connection to a neuron in the previous layer. The number 256 represents the number of neurons in the layer, and the activation parameter sets the activation function we want to use—in this case the ReLU function we saw earlier.

- A third layer of type Dense, also with 256 neurons fully connected to the second layer and again activated with a ReLU function.

- A fourth layer of type Dense, but in this case with only 10 neurons (one for each category) and an activation function of type softmax, therefore providing an output of 10 numbers that add up to 1.0, representing the probability of the input belonging to each class.

We are almost there! We can now train this neural network using the training dataset:

```
model.compile(optimizer='adam', loss='sparse_categorical_crossentropy',
        metrics=['accuracy'])
model.fit(x_train, y_train, epochs=4)
```

The method `compile` configures the training process. The `optimizer` parameter specifies the method that will be used to optimize the weights of our neural network. Passing the string `'SGD'` will result in the use of the familiar stochastic gradient descent algorithm covered in the previous section. In our example, we will use the Adam optimizer, a variation of stochastic gradient descent. This optimizer, based on the concept of adapting the learning rate dynamically for each parameter, provides great results.

The `loss` parameter allows us to set the loss function we want for our training. Keras provides many popular loss functions, such as mean squared error for regressions and categorical cross-entropy for classifications (a measure of how different our predicted category probabilities are from the real ones).

The `metrics` parameter provides a set of metrics that we want to monitor while training our model. They don't have any impact on the training of the model, but they will help us evaluate how good the model is.

Once we have configured the training, we can launch it by calling the function `fit` with the number of epochs (the total number of passes through our entire training dataset) we want.

The output of this program shows the progress of the training on the screen. You will be able to see in real time how the model is being trained, reducing the loss function value and increasing the accuracy:

```
Epoch 1/4
60000/60000 [==============================] - 10s 161us/sample -
  loss: 0.2214 - acc: 0.9333
Epoch 2/4
60000/60000 [==============================] - 9s 148us/sample -
  loss: 0.0894 - acc: 0.9718
Epoch 3/4
60000/60000 [==============================] - 11s 182us/sample -
  loss: 0.0613 - acc: 0.9801
Epoch 4/4
60000/60000 [==============================] - 12s 197us/sample -
  loss: 0.0434 - acc: 0.9861
```

The final accuracy of the model is 98.61%, not bad at all for such a simple neural network! That accuracy is calculated on the training dataset, though, which is not fair because we trained the model using those instances. To calculate the accuracy on a different set of images we can use our test dataset:

```
val_loss, val_acc = model.evaluate(x_test, y_test)
print(val_acc)
```

This shows an accuracy of 97.38%, also not bad.

Let's now predict the digits for all 10,000 test images we have in our dataset:

```
predictions = model.predict(x_test)
print(predictions[0])
```

The first prediction is the following—it seems that the model clearly identifies this picture as a 7 (99.999995% probability):

```
[1.6916850e-09 1.2803213e-09 2.8419381e-08 7.8183831e-08 8.2409468e-11
 1.6211030e-10 4.3845038e-15 9.9999952e-01 9.3910331e-11 3.2909591e-07]
```

Let's visualize the picture behind this prediction to see whether it really looks like the digit 7:

```
plt.imshow(x_test[0], cmap=plt.cm.binary)
plt.show()
```

And there you go! Figure A-40 shows the image, clearly a number 7. Congratulations!

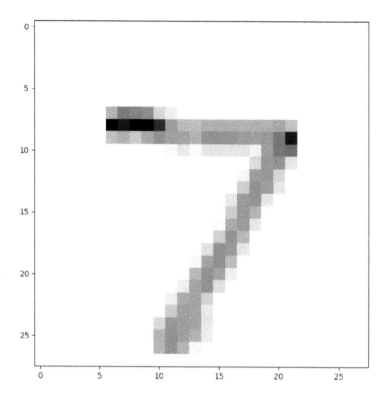

Figure A-40. Image categorized as a number 7 by our model

MORE NEURAL NETWORK ARCHITECTURES

Having all the layers fully connected is not always practical, as the number of weights grows very quickly as we increase the number of layers in our model. Other popular neural network architectures are the following:

Convolutional neural networks (CNNs)

These neural networks are particularly designed for computer vision tasks. They were inspired by how neurons are structured in the visual cortex: instead of being connected to the entire visual field, neurons in the visual cortex react only to a restricted region of the visual field called the *receptive field*. In the artificial neural network equivalent, nodes are connected to just a subset of the previous layer in a moving window that applies the same weights to the input, as shown in Figure A-41.

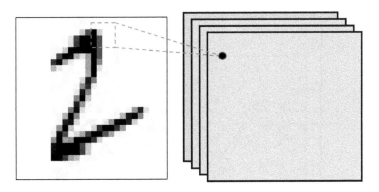

Figure A-41. Convolutional layer

Recurrent neural networks (RNNs)

In many cases, you will need to apply a neural network to a temporal sequence. Fully connected networks and convolutional networks are not useful for those scenarios because they take only the current input and don't keep history. Recurrent neural networks can consider not only the current input but also inputs from the past, connecting some nodes back to the input (as shown in Figure A-42). This is especially useful for scenarios such as speech recognition, for which the inputs from the past (e.g., initial words in a sentence) are useful for the current prediction (i.e., the current word being predicted).

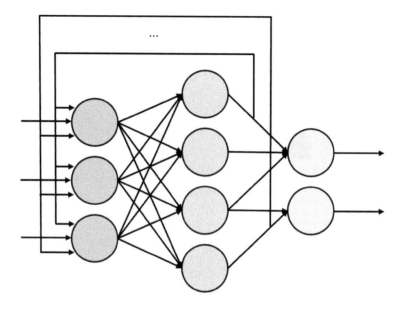

Figure A-42. Example of recurrent neural network

Long short-term memory (LSTM) networks

Regular recurrent neural networks can effectively only consider recent inputs from the past and are bad at considering inputs that occurred a long time ago. LSTM networks contain *memory cells* like the one shown in Figure A-43 that can keep information for a long period of time, and *gates* to set or forget the memory. LSTM networks are the most popular neural network architecture for speech recognition, speech synthesis, language translation, and autocompletion scenarios, among others.

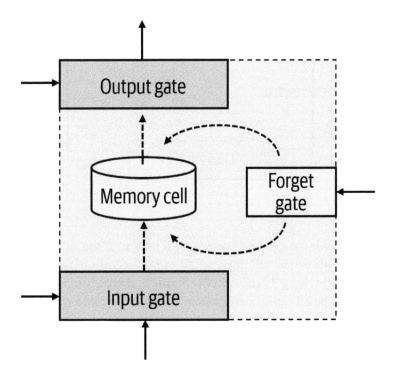

Figure A-43. Long short-term memory cell

Reinforcement Learning

"Greetings, Professor Falken. Shall we play a game?" If you've ever seen the movie *War Games* (*https://oreil.ly/AIO_A-17*), I'm sure you will remember that quote. It was the innocent greeting that a young hacker played by Matthew Broderick received when unwittingly accessing WOPR, an AI controlling the nuclear arsenal in the United States.

WOPR was originally programmed to predict possible outcomes of nuclear war, as well as to play the best strategy for an attack. Setting aside that the approach almost caused the entire human race to disappear from the planet, WOPR was a great example of using an exciting machine learning approach: *reinforcement learning.*

Reinforcement learning is one of the hottest topics in AI today. Instead of learning from data, it takes the approach of learning by *doing*. Figure A-44 shows the core components involved in this approach.

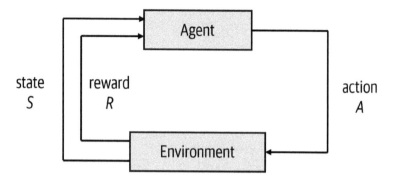

Figure A-44. Reinforcement learning

In every learning step, our AI, which we'll refer to as the *agent*, will perform an action (*A*). This action will cause an effect in the environment in which the agent operates, changing its state (*S*). For example, if our agent is a robotic arm, the action could be activating a servomotor and the state could be the position of the arm. If our agent is playing chess, the action would be moving a piece and the state is the position of all the pieces on the board.

For the agent to learn, we also add a third concept: the reward (*R*). After every action, we will reinforce positive outcomes and penalize negative outcomes. The reward will help the agent learn the appropriate actions for a given state, similarly to how babies learn how to crawl, walk, or demand attention from first-time parents (as some of you will know, after two or three kids the reward for demanding attention vanishes).

Learning by doing sounds amazing, and it really is. We don't need huge amounts of data, because the agent can learn by interacting with the environment directly. However, we won't usually be able to expose our agent to the real environment to play with it. If we did that, for WOPR to learn how to best defend its nation from a nuclear attack we would need to actually launch some nukes and provide good rewards for effective strategies—if we were still around to do that. For autonomous cars, the agent would need to crash thousands of real cars before learning how to drive safely.

For this reason, reinforcement learning is commonly used in conjunction with *simulation environments*. A simulation environment provides a playground for the agent to learn safely and at scale. Going back to *War Games*, WOPR learns how to defend from nuclear attacks (and play games like tic-tac-toe) through a fast-running simulation that it can play in a loop. In real-life scenarios, we use simulators such as Simulink (*https://oreil.ly/AIO_A-18*) (a multidomain simulator provided by the company MathWorks), Gym (*https://oreil.ly/AIO_A-19*) (a library provided by the organization OpenAI with prebuilt simulators for arcade games and robotics), or AirSim (*https://oreil.ly/AIO_A-20*) (a simulator provided by Microsoft for drones, cars, and other autonomous systems).

In this section, we will use OpenAI Gym as our simulator, which provides a CartPole environment (the equivalent of the "Hello, World" for reinforcement learning).

CARTPOLE EXAMPLE

To see the CartPole environment in action you first need to install OpenAI Gym, just like you've learned to do for other Python libraries:

```
python -m pip install --user gym
```

To initialize and render a CartPole environment we use the gym class provided by the library:

```
import gym

env = gym.make('CartPole-v0')
env.reset()
while True:
    env.render()
    env.step(env.action_space.sample())
env.close()
```

The code is pretty straightforward. After creating and initializing the CartPole environment with the methods make and reset, we just run an infinite loop in which we render the scene on the screen and perform a step applying a random action. Figure A-45 shows a frame of the resulting animation, before it quickly disappears from the screen.

Figure A-45. The CartPole environment

If we want to do more than just random actions in the environment, we need to understand what is happening in it first. The **step** function actually returns four values that will help us decide what action to take next:

observation
> An object representing the state of our environment. This could be the pixels on the screen or the joint angles of a robotic arm or the board state in a board game. In our case, **observation** will return an array with four elements describing the state of the cart pole: cart position, cart velocity, pole angle, and pole velocity at tip.

reward
> The amount of reward achieved by the action. The value also depends on the environment: in the case of the cart pole the reward will be +1 when the pole is upright.

done
> **true** if the episode has ended, which happens when the pole is more than a certain threshold from the vertical or the cart moves a certain distance from the center.

info
> Diagnostics information useful for debugging.

The `action` value will also be dependent on the environment. In our case it's very simple because it can have only two states: o for pushing the cart to the left, and 1 for pushing the cart to the right.

You can modify the previous program to show this information on screen and end the simulation when it's finished:

```
action = env.action_space.sample()
observation, reward, done, info = env.step(action)
print ("Action: ", action, "Observation: ", observation)
if done:
    break
```

The output will show something similar to this:

```
Action:  0 Observation:  [ 0.00746704 -0.16598137 -0.0481493   0.30460086]
Action:  0 Observation:  [ 0.00414742 -0.36038526 -0.04205729  0.58171832]
Action:  1 Observation:  [-0.00306029 -0.16470005 -0.03042292  0.27608886]
...
```

Q-LEARNING ALGORITHM

It's time for us to apply actions with some intelligence to keep the pole upright, instead of random values. The most common algorithm to do that is called *Q-Learning*, and it's behind many of the latest breakthroughs you've probably heard of on the news with AI beating humans at playing Atari games (*https://oreil.ly/ AIO_A-21*) or the ancient game of Go (*https://oreil.ly/AIO_A-22*).

The core concept behind Q-Learning is simpler than you may think. The idea is to define a table (called a Q-table) in which we will store values representing how good an action is for a given state. That value represents the *quality* of an action, hence the name Q-Learning.

Let's take a look at an example. Before almost annihilating the entire human race, WOPR also learned how to play tic-tac-toe. Its Q-table would look something like Table A-1 (TL=top left, MM=middle middle, BR=bottom right, and so on).

Table 9-1. Tic-tac-toe Q-table

Game state	TL	TM	TR	ML	ML	MR	BL	BM	BR
(board 1)	N/A	N/A	0.4	N/A	N/A	0.4	0.3	0.5	N/A
(board 2)	0.8	1	N/A	0.7	N/A	0.7	N/A	N/A	0.7
(board 3)	0.7	0.3	0.4	N/A	N/A	0.3	0.7	0.4	0.5
...	...	...	...	...	...	...	...	...	...

Each row represents a possible state in the game. In the case of tic-tac-toe, the rows contain each possible combination of markers on the board. Each column represents an action. In this case there are nine possible actions, each of them representing a move in a particular cell. Placing a marker in an occupied cell is of course not allowed in tic-tac-toe, hence the N/A values in some cells.

Playing tic-tac-toe is very simple for the machine if it has this table. For every move, it will just find the row that corresponds to the current state of the board and pick the action with the highest quality. The problem, though, is how do we calculate this magical table?

That's where the reward makes its appearance. We will define the quality of a move by how rewarding it is. The tricky part is that the reward may not be immediate. For example, in the case of tic-tac-toe we won't know if a move is good until the game finishes. Therefore, we have to define the quality as something like this:

Quality = instant reward + indication of future reward

Here's where things get interesting. Our indication of the future reward can be based on the quality of the resulting state. So, we decide where to move by considering the instant reward of making that move and how good the resulting state is.

This concept is the key ingredient of Q-Learning, and the magic behind most applications of reinforcement learning you will see out there, from Atari game-play to autonomous vehicles. The equation modeling this concept is called the *Bellman equation* and looks like this:

$$Q(s, a) = r + \gamma(max(Q(s', a')))$$

Let's go through the key elements in this equation:

- $Q(s,a)$ is the quality value we are calculating for a given state (s) and action (a). It's basically the cell we are calculating for a given move.

- r is the instant reward that we achieve by performing that action a in the current state s. In the case of a tic-tac-toe game, we could define it as a positive value if we win the game with that move, negative if we lose it, and zero if the game doesn't finish with the move.

- $max(Q(s', a'))$ is the maximum quality of the resulting state s'. We calculate it by taking the highest value in the row corresponding to the state we move to after applying our action.

- γ is called the *discount factor*. It allows us to model how much importance to give to future rewards versus immediate rewards. A high value will prioritize future rewards, and a low value will prioritize short-term outcomes instead.

Now that you know the basic math behind Q-Learning, you can create a program that *learns* how to play tic-tac-toe by repeatedly playing the game. The steps involved are the following:

1. For each game played (also called an *episode*), record the entire sequence of moves and the outcome (win, loss, draw).

2. Assign a reward to the last move the machine makes as its quality value in the Q-table. For example, you can assign +1 for a win, 0 for a draw, and –1 for a loss.

3. For each previous move, update its quality value using the Bellman equation. Note that we are using a parameter a called the *learning rate*. Without

a learning rate we would replace the Q-value entirely in each episode. What if the human made a mistake in this game? The machine would learn the wrong lesson. We want it to learn gradually in each iteration, which we can achieve by using an a value between 0 and 1:

$$Q(s,a) = (1 - a) \cdot Q(s, a) + a \cdot \gamma \cdot (max(Q(s', a')))$$

The actual code is beyond the scope of this book, but I encourage you to take a look at some implementations by the community, such as the one by Carsten Friedrich in GitHub (*https://oreil.ly/AIO_A-23*). His project contains multiple implementations of different strategies for playing tic-tac-toe, including the Q-Learning technique you just learned. The chart in Figure A-46 shows the progression of a training session.

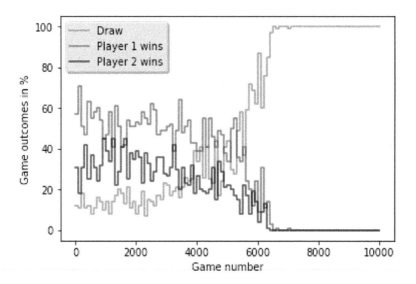

Figure A-46. Tic-tac-toe training

You can see how our Q-Learning algorithm is able to learn how to play tic-tac-toe in about 6,000 games. Playing 6,000 games against a machine can be very boring, but we can easily fix that inconvenience by making the computer play against itself. In the previous example, the chart corresponds to a training session between two instances of the same algorithm.

Just like in the final scene of *War Games*, after playing thousands of games and learning how to master tic-tac-toe by itself, you can see that the only possible outcome is a draw. To quote WOPR in the most memorable moment in the movie: "A strange game. The only winning move is not to play. How about a nice game of chess?"

DEEP Q-LEARNING

As simple and elegant as the Q-Learning approach might be, it is not applicable to most real-world scenarios. Computers can easily manage the number of possible states in a tic-tac-toe game (about 250,000), but as soon as we move to other games the Q-table can turn into something humongous. For example, applying the same technique to a game of chess would involve a table with approximately 10^{43} rows, one for each potential board state. That would be the equivalent of several quintillion times the current data volume stored in the world today. The game of Go is even more complex and gets to an order of magnitude of 10^{170}—I'm pretty sure you won't be able to afford the hard drive required to store that table!

To make things even more difficult, consider the steering wheel in an autonomous vehicle, or the angle of a robot articulation. Both the state and the action can be continuous values instead of discrete numbers, something we can't model easily with a Q-table.

This is where Deep Q-Learning comes in handy. Instead of storing every possible Q-value in a table, Deep Q-Learning creates a function that approximates that table. What technique have you learned already to do that in a powerful way? That's right, our beloved neural networks can provide a solution to this problem.

With Deep Q-Learning we don't store a Q-table anymore. Every time we calculate a new Q-value for a particular state and a particular action, we will use that combination as a training input to our neural network. Once we have done enough episodes of training the neural network will be able to correctly estimate the Q-values by itself, deciding what action to perform next. As an additional bonus, this approach can work perfectly with both actions and states that are continuous instead of discrete.

Let's put this brilliant idea to work in our original scenario, balancing the cart pole. If you still remember, the state of our CartPole environment was defined by four continuous values (cart position, cart velocity, pole angle, and pole velocity at tip), which makes it perfect for the Deep Q-Learning technique.

You can find several Deep Q-Learning implementations developed by the community on GitHub. For our example we will use one by Greg Surma (*https:// oreil.ly/AIO_A-24*). All the action is happening in one file, *cartpole.py*. If you look at the code closely you will find the following fragment as part of the class DQNSolver:

```
self.model = Sequential()
self.model.add(Dense(24, input_shape=(observation_space,),
            activation="relu"))
self.model.add(Dense(24, activation="relu"))
self.model.add(Dense(self.action_space, activation="linear"))
self.model.compile(loss="mse", optimizer=Adam(lr=LEARNING_RATE))
```

That piece of code should already be familiar to you—it's initializing the neural network that will do all the magic. It's a very simple network, with three fully connected layers. The neural network is designed with as many inputs as there are observations (four, in our case: cart position, cart velocity, pole angle, and pole velocity at tip) and as many outputs as there are actions (two in our case: pushing left and pushing right). For more advanced environments, you will work with other neural network architectures, including recurrent neural networks, LSTM neural networks, and convolutional neural networks.

No matter what architecture you use, the neural network will identify the next action to perform at every step. The code for this is also part of the class DQNSolver, and it's pretty straightforward:

```
def act(self, state):
    if np.random.rand() < self.exploration_rate:
        return random.randrange(self.action_space)
    q_values = self.model.predict(state)
    return np.argmax(q_values[0])
```

The first two lines add some random exploration to the execution, so the system can also explore new actions while learning. By calling the method `predict` (which you're already familiar with) we will predict the Q-values for all actions of the passed state. Finally, we return the action with the maximum Q-value, which will be the one we will perform.

The core code for the training is invoked in every step by replaying a random batch of the previous steps and looks like this:

```
for state, action, reward, state_next, terminal in batch:
    q_update = reward
    if not terminal:
```

```
q_update = (reward + \
        GAMMA * np.amax(self.model.predict(state_next)[0]))
q_values = self.model.predict(state)
q_values[0][action] = q_update
self.model.fit(state, q_values, verbose=0)
```

For each move we update the Q-value using the formula you are familiar with, and we call the fit method of our neural network model to train it.

The result is quite spectacular to watch. You will see how the system learns in every episode, keeping the pole upright for longer and longer on each iteration. I encourage you to replicate the code on your computer and experience it for yourself, but if you're feeling lazy or don't have the time right now Figure A-47 shows the learning process. The y-axis represents the number of steps for which the system is able to maintain the pole in an upright position. As the number of episodes increases you can see how the system is able to keep the pole upright for a longer time.

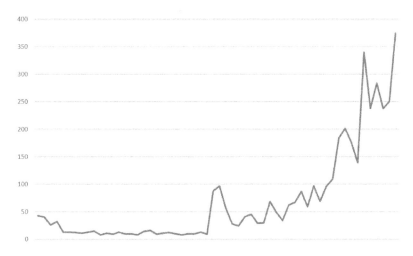

Figure A-47. Learning process for the cart pole task

Learn More

In this special *Undercover Boss: Technical Edition*, you have learned the basics of the main technologies behind AI. I'm not expecting you to host an all hands meeting like in the TV show, but hopefully this has helped you understand the core concepts and techniques required to implement AI solutions.

I encourage you to not stop here. As you've seen, to drive the AI transformation, not only do the technical units need to come closer to the business, but the business leaders need to come closer to the technology. Here are some resources that can help bridge that gap:

- Microsoft AI School (*https://oreil.ly/AIO_A-25*)
- Azure AI Engineer Associate certification (*https://oreil.ly/AIO_A-26*)
- Machine Learning (*https://oreil.ly/AIO_A-27*) and Deep Learning (*https://oreil.ly/AIO_A-28*) courses at Coursera by Andrew Ng

Remember that AI heroes are constantly reinventing themselves. Who knows, maybe after learning about AI techniques you may decide to reinvent yourself—there's always room for new AI developers!

Index

About the Author

David Carmona manages Microsoft AI's go-to-market and strategy across enterprise and developer AI products, services, and innovation. David has more than two decades of experience in the technology industry where he began his career as a software engineer. He joined Microsoft more than 15 years ago and has held a variety of technical and business leadership roles both internationally and in Redmond.

O'REILLY®

There's much more where this came from.

Experience books, videos, live online training courses, and more from O'Reilly and our 200+ partners—all in one place.

Learn more at oreilly.com/online-learning